...lyn Nuttall is thirty-three-years old and is living in London ..., six years after the attack that nearly cost her her life. ...re the attack, Merlyn was a fashion designer for one of the ...st retailing groups in the UK. In 1997 she started her own ...on business which, after less than a year in operation, is ...ving. Merlyn also works closely with Victim Support, on a ...tary basis, as a spokesperson and adviser on victims' needs.

IT COULD HAVE BEEN YOU

Merlyn Nuttall

with

Sharon Morrison

LEWISHAM	
Bertrams	31.08.06
362.883	£6.99
814661	/

A *Virago* Book

Published by Virago Press 1998
Reprinted 2000

First published in Great Britain in 1997
by Virago Press

A CIP catalogue record for this book
is available from the British Library

ISBN 1 86049 368 8

Typeset in Garamond by M Rules
Printed and bound in Great Britain by
Clays Ltd, St Ives plc

Virago
A Division of
Little, Brown and Company (UK)
Brettenham House
Lancaster Place
London WC2E 7EN

Contents

To my sister Sharon,
and in memory of Mum and Dad –
the most wonderful parents in the world

Acknowledgements

I want to thank so many people for the overwhelming support, practical help, compassion and advice they have given me over the past five years. I could not have survived without them.

Family

I am blessed to have a family with such gargantuan heart: my eldest sister, Loraine Crook, and my nephew Daniel; my youngest sister, Lesley Nuttall, and her boyfriend Pat Sheehan; my nieces and nephew, Merlyn, Jenny and Richard Morrison, for the continuing joy they bring me; my stepmother, Myra Bancroft, and her husband Brian, my loving army of uncles, aunts and cousins who are too many to name individually – I thank you all for reminding me that I belong to a big family that will always be there when needed. A special mention for my brother-in-law, John. Thank you for welcoming me into your home for all these years, and for all your input on the book.

Friends

My stalwarts who were there for me at my darkest moments and stuck with me through to my brightest times. Valerie, Simon Gregory, Tony Charalambous, Chip Harris, Heather Jackson, Sakina and Dan O'Neil, Chantelle Morton, Ilgi and David Spilsbury, Madeleine Hazard, Ali Taghavi, Sharon Cotwal, Barbara Horspool, Angela Tysler, Paula Gaskell, Sarah Kingsbury, Sandy, Peter, Robert, Joan and Alf Nicholls, Angela Murgatroyde, Danny Abrahamovitos, Sirma Koro, Sue Chorley and Pete Fish, David Bowen, Mark Nicholson, Alan Richards, Cliff Homow, Helen and Mark Dorion, Maggie and Don Ellison, Wendy and David Hulton, Anthony and Stella Good and especially Andrew Bignell who holds my heart.

In memory of Felix Martin-Reyes and Doyle Richmond.

For being my beacons of light when the gloom closed in: Anna Hunter and Julie Chimes-Law.

Christina Tattari for the superb work she has done on my scars, not only physical but mental. Professor Cawley and all at Charter Nightingale Hospital – he allowed me to be myself and believe in myself. The community of Gibraltar that welcomed me, especially John at Kingsley Hay. Marian and Bill Fitzpatrick for all their medical help and advice. Bill Massey. Carmel Perry and Chris Kay.

National Health Service

Dr Ruth Brown for her care in Casualty. Dr Graham Buckley and Mr Manuel Oyarzabal for the initial work they did on my wounds. Dr Horton for his sensitivity and common sense.

Acknowledgements

The Police

Everyone at Brixton Police Station, but especially the team in the Incident Room who put their heart and soul into the investigation. A very special thanks to WPC Nicola Holding, DC Mark Chapman and DSI John Jones (retired).

The Firemen

Brixton Red Watch, especially Ian Crittenden who literally held my life together.

Employers

Bhs, whose planning and understanding eased my financial worries and smoothed my way back into working life.

The Judiciary

John Nutting QC for the wonderful case he argued for the prosecution. Helena Kennedy QC for her representation of me pro-bono – I can never thank you enough. Terry Lee and Evill and Coleman Solicitors for their continuing help and advice.

Support Agencies

Victim Support for giving me a platform to speak from, and Helen Peggs for all her help.

BT for the loan of their mobile phone.
British Midland for their understanding.

Preface

There has only ever been one objective in writing this book: to enable other victims of sexual assault to deal successfully with what has happened to them on an emotional and a practical level.

Since the first publication of *It Could Have Been You*, I have been overwhelmed by the positive response it has triggered among fellow survivors, their families and friends and support groups. It has reinforced my belief that you do not need limitless reserves of inner strength, courage or money, just an innate sense that what happened to you was wrong, was not your fault and that your assailant must be prevented from raping again.

I count my blessings every day. I have the continuing, solid support of my own family and friends, and the love of my partner, Andrew. In July 1997 I opened my own dress agency, in partnership with Andrew. I'm working back in fashion again, living in the city I adore and with the man I love.

For a brief moment in time I was a victim; I became a survivor.

Merlyn Nuttall, 1998

Foreword

I remember reading the newspaper reports of Merlyn Nuttall's case and having an intake of breath. The details were so shocking that all my years of experience did not reduce the sense of horror and outrage that I felt. A woman is dragged off the street at knifepoint in broad daylight, sexually assaulted, cut up, garotted and left to be burnt alive. It engaged with my worst nightmares. That one human being should subject another to such violation and humiliation, and wreak such havoc upon her life, filled me with incomprehension and anger.

The perpetrator, Anthony Ferrira, was eventually brought to justice and dealt with by the courts. In passing sentence the judge spoke of Merlyn's extraordinary courage and will to survive. It is that determination and strength which impresses everyone who has contact with her, and when I met her it bowled me over too.

Some months after reading about the trial, I received a telephone call from friends who worked in television. They had met Merlyn when working on a programme about her case and had clearly been deeply affected by her experience. They explained to me that she had embarked upon a claim for compensation before the Criminal Injuries Compensation Board but was finding the procedures byzantine and unsympathetic. They wondered if there was anything I could do.

Legal Aid is not available for tribunals or boards. The original principle was that the procedures should be straightforward so that people would be able to put their case without the need for a lawyer. Unfortunately, as the rules have become more developed and the method of calculating an award has acquired more peculiarities, many applicants find themselves floundering in a welter of demands when they are often still reeling from the effects of the crime.

At the time, I was particularly exercised by the issue of criminal compensation because the government had just introduced a tariff scheme. This meant that people would receive compensation within tightly prescribed bands instead of allowing the Board to determine how much an applicant should receive on the basis of individual loss, pain and suffering. The new scheme was clearly a cost-cutting exercise.

For some time I had been arguing for the Board to make more generous awards to victims of sexual assault because they were rarely able to sue their attacker yet the effects of the trauma lived with them for years. The Board would readily accept medical evidence of physical injury and loss of earnings and would be prepared to compensate for measurable loss but was often unprepared to acknowledge less tangible consequences. Any of us who worked with rape victims knew about the long-term effects on relationships, self-esteem, even the ability to go out. The Board had slowly been shifting to a greater acceptance of psychological suffering. However, the new tariff system meant victims of rape and other brutal offences would be compensated on a wholly inadequate scale.

There is no compensation for the ordeal of violent crime. Nothing can ever completely return the victim to the way they were before the event. Something is lost forever. However, a proper recognition of the damage and loss is crucial to recovery. Although it is impossible to put a financial value on a victim's suffering, that should not prevent us attempting some kind of restorative justice.

I met Merlyn at my chambers with the solicitor who was acting for her. When she recounted to me the details of her experience, I was appalled. All the lessons I have learned in the courtroom about the nature of such desperate violence against women never dull the reality when I hear it first hand.

I told Merlyn that I would happily argue the case for her before the Board without payment and we would pull out the stops to get her a proper level of compensation. Because Merlyn's case pre-dated the change in the regulations, she would be able to make her application under the old rules, which meant she was at least not restricted to a low level tariff rate. However, the operation of the system even in its original form places extra difficulties in the way of rape victims. This includes not only the fact that applicants cannot claim the cost of legal representation, but there is also often a delay in getting the case heard which is enormously stressful. The process can also be quite humiliating because it involves the disclosure of such intimate matters and can involve the inspection of injuries by Board members who are invariably men of a certain age.

The amount of compensation which rape victims are awarded shows a great deal of variance. The following case judgements illustrate that the Board can make a moral judgement on the applicant which may have nothing to do with the facts of the case. A woman who was a prostitute was subjected to a terrible life-threatening sexual assault. She was subject to attempted buggery, threats to kill, forced oral sex and violence. She suffered multiple abrasions to her face and neck, rope burns to her wrists and swelling and bruising of her buttocks. Not surprisingly, she had psychological problems including nightmares, loss of self-esteem, inability to form sexual relationships and fears of being alone. Having been clear of heroin abuse for years, she returned to her former addiction. The award was £1,700 which was later increased on appeal to £6,500 (Case of Saunders, May 1993). There was no doubt that the level of compensation was lower because the victim was considered less worthy because of her 'character'.

Merlyn was not going to be handicapped in this way. No one could claim she was the author of her own misfortune or in any way unworthy but the fact that such factors do affect the outcome is wholly objectionable.

Reviewing the level of awards for rape was itself shocking. General Damages for horrifying rapes were usually in the region of £10,000 and where they were greater there was evidence that the woman was completely broken by the trauma and unlikely to recover.

The following case histories are from the law reports.

A thirty-year-old woman (thirty-four at the date of the hearing) was subjected to a vicious sexual assault by a friend of her husband. The assault lasted two hours during which time she was forced at knife-point to participate in oral sex. She was struck and stabbed several times resulting in two superficial wounds, requiring four stitches. She recovered quickly from the physical injuries but developed depression, anxiety, personality change and exacerbation of pre-existing asthma. She attempted suicide in 1983 and could no longer live a normal life. She continued to suffer from nightmares, was unable to live alone, panicked if she was left alone with a man. The prognosis was poor: she was unlikely to form a normal relationship with a man, would be prone to depression and continuing asthma (which was exacerbated due to the problems). *S. v Meah – July 1986*

General damages: £10,000 (£15,000 as at January 1995).

A twenty-two-year-old woman was raped in a well-lit urban area at night. Her cries for help went unheeded. She received blows to the face and stomach and was threatened with murder. She believed that the assailant had a knife and would use it. She sustained no physical injuries. However she had faced psychological symptoms over two years and would continue to do so. These included distrust of society and men in particular (meaning that there was no interest in any level of relationship), unease in travelling alone, a change in personality to a more timid and introverted person. There was no psychiatric evidence as to when the psychiatric problems may cease. *Re X – January 1990*

General damages: £10,000 (12,500 as at January 1995).

A woman, aged twenty when raped (twenty-two at the date of the hearing), sustained bruising to her ribs. She suffered from psychological symptoms: depression, anxiety, nightmares, weight loss and sexual dysfunction. She was off work for one month and broke up with her boyfriend soon after the rape. At the time of the hearing she had married and her condition improved, although she continued to suffer from recurrent depression, anxiety and was unable to remain home due to fear of attack. *Re Farley – January 1993*

General damages: £9,000 (£9,720 as at January 1995).

A female, aged thirty-nine at the date of rape (forty-two at the date of hearing), was raped twice by her husband. She sustained hip and arm injuries. She suffered psychological problems, being nervous, exhausted, fearful of social situations especially with men, she lacked confidence and self-esteem, was disorientated and unable to continue social activities. She was fearful of violence after her husband was released from prison. *Re X – May 1992*

General damages: £25,000 (including £5,000 for physical injuries) (£27,500 as at January 1995).

At Merlyn's hearing, we presented a wealth of evidence about her loss of earnings, the physical and psychological effects of the crime, the cost of plastic surgery to repair the wounds, the terror she still experienced. I was conscious of the appalling irony: that Merlyn's efforts towards her own recovery would reduce the award she would finally receive. Appearing before the Board was a beautiful young woman, a survivor, and it would strangely count against her in the lottery of compensation.

As it transpired, in 1995 Merlyn received £76,000 in total, the highest award a rape victim had ever received up to that point. Her General Damages, that is the amount for pain and suffering, was £30,000. The rest was for loss of earnings, medical and other *actual* costs. We celebrated a victory, but I went home thinking of the *Coronation Street* actor who was awarded libel damages of £50,000 for the insult of being described as a bore.

The press made the point that, had Merlyn's rape been subject to the new tariff regime, she would probably have been awarded £7,000.

The introduction of the tariff scheme was challenged in the courts by the trade unions. By a decision of the Judicial Committee of the House of Lords on 5 April 1995, the means by which the Home Secretary, Michael Howard, had introduced the new scheme was held to be unlawful. He had not even bothered to put the changes through Parliament. Consequently, the new scheme was withdrawn.

However, the struggle to obtain justice for injured women goes on. The challenge is to bring the reality of women's experience into the law and to create a system which vigilantly protects both defendents' rights, and those of the victim.

Merlyn Nuttall wrote her book so that we would begin to understand what it is like to experience this kind of crime. Her story reinforces the problems which exist within the Criminal Justice System, even where the key players – police, lawyers, judges – are doing their level best to be more sensitive. We still have a long way to go. Her account will add another piece to the body of knowledge which is changing the legal system. For that she deserves our gratitude as well as our admiration.

Helena Kennedy, QC

CHAPTER 1

The Attack

He was black. His hair was cropped into a fashionable flat top and he was wearing a smart blue tracksuit. There was a clean-cut look about him, but his eyes were bulging and he was clearly agitated. He appeared suddenly from an entrance to a row of dilapidated houses. I was unaware of his presence until a voice coming from my right called out, 'Excuse me!' He was waving his arms animatedly. 'Please, please help me! My girl-friend's pregnant. She's fallen – could you stay with her while I get an ambulance?'

I stopped, slightly irritated. Yet I could not believe there was anything sinister in his appearance. After all, I reasoned, it wasn't dark but broad daylight – and the place, even at seven in the morning, was humming with people and traffic. I pulled my sleeve back to look at my watch, almost mechanically, and was just about to suggest that he let me call for an ambulance or doctor, when suddenly he was at my side. He grabbed hold of my arm with his left hand and showed the blade of a knife with his right. I froze. I couldn't believe this was happening. I'd never been confronted with anything like a knife before. I didn't know what to think or do. That brief glance I had had of him when he first called to me was to be the only serious look I would have throughout the deadly minutes that followed. From this time he ensured either that he was behind me, or that I would not dare to turn my head to look.

He said softly but firmly that I was to do as he said. I felt the knife pressing into the thickness of my clothing and I mentally freaked. 'Hurry,' he said. 'She's alone . . .' I was stunned, yet somehow hoping for the best, refusing to accept his intentions might be evil. Despite the knife, I thought that it was only his anxiety for the safety of the girl that had made him do this. My heart seemed to stop as he pushed the knife into my coat. The thought of running or screaming or fighting never entered my head and I don't believe I could have done any of those things anyway.

All of this must have taken a few seconds, yet all I could do was say to myself, 'Stay calm. He's desperate – he's only desperate.' With traffic pounding a few yards away, it was already so unreal. Surely someone must have seen what was happening? It was only four or five yards to the pathway leading to the three-storey house. His body was close to my back and his grip on my arm was like a vice. He forced me towards the house at the furthest end of the terrace, set back from the others. Dustbins had spilled out their waste: old bottles, rusted springs and piles of ashes littered the tiny forecourt. We stumbled up nine steps to the house. The doorway with its peeling paintwork was flanked by two round columns and was ajar. Several windows were hung with dirty, torn nets. Inside it was dark and squalid. The smell was overpowering. It was pungent, a mixture of stale vomit and urine. I had never been in such a place before.

Wallpaper was hanging from the walls, there was no floor- or stair-covering. Junk was strewn everywhere.

Even then I still hoped he was simply a desperate man, a hope that I clung to as I stumbled and he continued to shout, 'Hang on, honey, I've brought someone,' all the way up the five flights of stairs to the attic. There, he positioned himself on the landing, holding me tightly against him. His foot came round and kicked the door open. 'In there,' he commanded. There was no girlfriend inside, pregnant or otherwise. There was no one at all. This realisation sent jolts of panic thudding through me. I half turned and, finding my voice, I screamed, 'No! No!' and pushed to get by him and out. It was an eerie feeling: a mixture of terror and frantic despair.

But *he* was there blocking my way. Although he was about my height and build he assumed the proportions of a colossus. He also had the advantage of knowing I was petrified, isolated and totally in his power. His hands went round my neck and I struggled to breathe. His fingers tightened and black spots flashed in front of my eyes as my legs buckled at the knees. He was now pulling my scarf tighter and tighter, strangling me. I began to choke and fought for air. I wanted to kick out but I could not move. Visions of my sister and her daughter, my god-daughter, flashed across my mind. I didn't want to die. Not like this! Not in a place like this! It all seemed to be in slow motion. He released the pressure as suddenly as he had applied it. I coughed and gulped and staggered. His head was close to the back of mine as he whispered, 'No one can hear you up here.' My terror increased. I knew he was right.

My eyes darted everywhere. My brain was trying to come to terms with the situation. The room was small. There were two skylights in the sloping ceiling, blackened out by fabric that was pinned to them. A bed with dirty covers was opposite the door. There was a low, rickety table and a dark-coloured typist's chair. The only light came from a lamp in the corner of the room. Incongruously, a green plastic Harrods carrier bag lay on top of a heap of rubbish, and there were old rags in the corner.

He told me to do as he ordered: to look at the wall. I must always look towards the wall, never move unless he said so, and never, never turn to look at him. As I stood shaking in front of him he told me to take off my overcoat, but before I could do this he pushed me face down on to the bed and was tugging at the jacket I was wearing under it. My panic increased when his pulling pinned my arms momentarily inside the sleeves. He pulled more urgently and both coats dropped on to the grubby floor. He snatched at my T-shirt and I felt his nails claw my back. Then, incredibly, he stopped and said that he liked my palazzo pants. My brain raced to comprehend his swings of mood, from friendly conversation, as if everything was normal, to sudden attack. Perhaps, I thought, I can reason with him, humour him. I was already thinking of survival.

He pounced again, tearing away at my underwear. He seemed to have some trouble with my bra fastening, literally ripping it from me. Yet he took my shoes off gently and, dropping the bra, said, 'I like the shoes. Where did you buy them, what make are they?'

'They're Shelly shoes,' I replied in a trembling voice. The weirdness of his remarks only terrified me more. I lay face down on the bed in that dim and chillingly cold room without a stitch of clothing on. My senses strained at every movement, every noise. I could hear him moving around, shuffling. He asked me whether I had a boyfriend. I said, untruthfully, 'Yes.' Then he wanted to know how old I was. 'Twenty-seven,' I said.

'What date?' he asked.

'The seventeenth of October, 1964,' I replied. Perhaps he's

only going to beat me up and steal my credit cards – he would need my date of birth for that, I reasoned.

'What do you do?' he asked. I could feel his eyes on me.

'I'm a fashion buyer,' I replied weakly, aware how lame this whole conversation was. The sense of disbelief was overbearing. I was impatient even, if that was possible, to see where all this was going, to get it over with and, most of all, to get out.

But this strange and incredible discussion carried on. He was standing now at the bottom of the bed looking down at me. I could not see more than his legs – they were now bare; he was already undressed at least from the waist down. I was icy cold and trembling. My Filofax had fallen on to the bed during the first struggle and was now next to me. I fixed my gaze on it . . . and waited.

A voice in my head then said to try humouring him. If I could keep up a dialogue . . . I asked if he had done this kind of thing before, and he said he hadn't, that I was the first. So I asked him, 'Why me?'

'Because I couldn't get a pretty girl like you the ordinary way,' he replied.

He then moved away from the bed and I was desperate to know what he was doing. I heard a clink and smelled whisky. I breathed in deeply but couldn't detect any other smells. I didn't know what he was doing . . . taking drugs? Subsequently I found out he was on a mixture of crack and cocaine which is familiarly known as a 'spitbomb'. I was also later to learn that he claimed he needed drugs to achieve sexual satisfaction, and that he had killed another man. Had I been aware of any of this at the time of the attack I am not sure that I would have been able to react in the way that I did, and fight for life: I suppose I was helped by thinking that I was the first person he had ever done this to and therefore I stood a chance.

The drugs had an immediate effect. He told me to move up the bed.

I had had several boyfriends in my life, and physical contact had always been associated with mutual affection and trust. I had experienced the joy of reciprocating touch and feelings and respect for each other. It matched the understanding I had always had of relationships throughout my upbringing. I didn't know what to expect now or how to cope. I felt inadequate, ashamed of my body being on exhibition and cripplingly afraid of him. I was confused and suddenly dehumanised.

He told me what he wanted and how he wanted it. I could sense him close to the bed looking down at me as he told me to perform sexual acts on myself so he could watch. I just could not do it. I went rigid and he went into a rage.

'Turn over and keep looking at the wall,' he bellowed. He got on top of me and I knew I was about to be buggered. I could feel his closeness and trembled uncontrollably. I jerked away, clawing at the bedclothes and holding my head at an awkward angle to avoid seeing him, in fear of angering him more.

'Please! No, not that!' I wailed.

To my amazement he stopped. He got off the bed and said calmly, 'OK, but if I'm not to have that, you will have to give me something else I want.'

I could feel my heart pumping away: it was throbbing in my head. There was an awful damp, musty smell coming from the bed and mattress. What was he going to do to me now? He wanted me to bite him and make him come. I shut my eyes and didn't move an inch. I was completely traumatised. I knew I could not do as he wanted. So he forced it, saying, 'You must hate me. Why can't you bite it?' He was not agitated now. All his movements were made with calm deliberation. He turned me over, then clambered on the bed and knelt on my shoulders, pinning me down. I smelled his skin and body odour and tried to blot his presence from my mind, concentrating on a word written across his chest, 'hummel', forcing myself to say that this did not matter, yet knowing with all my heart that it did. He completed his act in a series of jerking movements. 'Swallow it, swallow it!' he screamed, then jumped off the bed and leaned over me. 'Turn over and look at the wall,' he said. My stomach churned; my head ached. I felt dead inside my soul.

I don't know whether I was relieved that the rape was over and that I had survived it, or whether I was already apprehensive about what was to happen next. I heard the sound of his dressing. He would let me go now that he had had what he wanted.

'Can I go to work now – I'm late for my meeting?' I asked simply. How stupid and unreal that sounds now! Yet at the time it was a question of hope and one that I thought might calm him down.

He didn't answer. Instead he asked me to pass him a plastic bag that was on the floor beyond my head, and to do it without looking around. But I did look round this time, slightly turning my head to the right. At the angle I lay, I could see that he was dressed in his tracksuit and was fumbling inside the bag. He brought out what appeared to be a wire with bamboo handles on each end. It looked like cheese wire. I wondered why the hell he was carrying cheese wire in a bag . . . and still I thought he would let me go.

The mattress dipped and I knew he was kneeling on the bed beside me, over me. I felt something being slipped over my head and around my throat. My scarf? String? I wanted to believe it was anything but cheese wire. The wire bit into my neck and I felt pain the like of which I had never known before, sharp, searing, tearing away at me, and blocking off my breathing. Waves of shock and pain hit every part of my being.

I knew then that he was going to kill me. That he had always intended to kill me. That it didn't matter who I was. He was out to rape and kill that day, and that was that. I reeled from the impact of this realisation. I had been raped, beaten, throttled in his fury, yet I had always hoped he didn't intend to take my life as well. Now there was no more pretence.

Then it was as if something occurred within me that gave me a surge of energy. I could not, would not die like this. I wanted to see my little niece grow up more than anything in the world. I wanted the closeness of my sisters more than I had ever wanted it before and nothing, but nothing, mattered as much as that. These were my priorities. No others existed. This must all have happened in an instant for I instinctively put my hands up and under the wire to pull it away. He pulled harder and the pain made me scream high and loud and long, as the wire cut into the thumb joint on my right hand, almost severing it. Yet none of his frenzy diminished the fight I suddenly had in me. He would not take my life from me as well. 'No, he will not,' I kept saying to myself, again and again and again.

I struggled and flailed with my legs and pummelled with my other arm, aware of the intense pain and praying for it to stop. We rolled off the bed on to the floor in the fight, and I know I hit my head against something but I was numb to the pain now.

He slackened the hold with the wire and pulled it away from my throat, tearing at the skin, jerking my chin up. I suppose I must have looked close to death, but he was not finished with me. He straddled my body, punching and kicking, leaving no part of my body untouched. In my despair I kept trying to hit back. Then I let out a sob of anguish. He had a new weapon, a broken bottle. (I later found out that he had used it to inhale his drugs.) He grabbed hold of me from behind and with his arm over my shoulder hacked and jabbed it into my throat. I pushed back against him but could not get away from him. My constant pulling away and tugging at him with my fingers broke my nails but he couldn't get a straight jab at my windpipe. The hacking and stabbing went on and on, tearing into my larynx. We twisted round and round in that room and it was, to me, as if it was the only place in the universe. People were walking and traffic was moving just a matter of yards away, but it was as if we were on another planet, away from humanity and civilisation. My head started to pound. There was an acute whirling sensation as if I was being spun around faster and faster. I just wanted it to stop, this intense pain in my head. The light was getting weaker and weaker, and red and black blotches clashed together in front of my eyes. I cannot remember breathing, or noise, or anything as I asked myself, 'Is this death? Is this what it is going to be like for ever and ever? Stop. Please let this stop!'

I could feel the dirty floorboards beneath me and was aware that life was slipping away. Everything that I held dear flashed again through my consciousness. Now he was hacking away at the back of my neck, carving criss-cross imprints of the jagged bottle just under my skull, at the nape of my neck. I must have lost consciousness then.

I don't know how long I was out. When I came round I was aware of the searing pain and throbbing in my hand. My eyes focused hazily on it: the thumb was lying at a peculiar angle to the rest of the hand. I felt nothing from my throat or neck except a vague soreness. Nor did I realise that I was bleeding or in fact how much blood I had lost, even though it was spattered around the room, on the bed and all over me. I simply did not see it. I did not move as my ears strained to detect noise. He was still in the room, moving around, and I steeled myself. But another shock hit me as I recognised the sound of fire crackling, then the physical sensation of fire, of heat and of a burning pain. Oh my God – he's setting me alight! He had put my clothes by my head and feet and set them on fire. My heel was burning so I instinctively moved it. He reacted at once to this sign of life and hit out, beating and kicking and hacking again at the back of my exposed neck with the bottle.

I knew that if I was to survive, I had to feign death now. The miracle of it all was that the adrenaline did not cease to flow, the mental determination to fight and survive did not waver and, with only one or two exceptions, my brain remained alert enough to reason. By some strange chance my memory locked on to the words spoken in jest by my swimming tutor when I was a child. I was frightened to breathe in the water, so I would hold my breath while I swam whole lengths, and she always joked about my lung capacity. Now I looked to that as the only key to life. I must not move a muscle, no matter what he did or how much the fire burned my skin. I held my breath when he leaned over me again, and when he gave me a push I remained still, rolling easily to his prodding. It seemed an eternity before I dared open my eyes and focus or analyse sounds. When I did, the room was empty. He was gone.

The room was filling with black and acrid smoke, especially from the mattress. I pulled myself to my feet, swayed, stabilised, and hobbled to the door. The door knob wasn't there. I was locked in!

I pounded the door, but my yells were weak and the harder I tried to make a noise, the more my brain was telling me that nothing was happening. Was noise coming out? I just didn't know. The smoke was getting denser, stinging my eyes. Panic and frustration set in.

I pulled the rag away from the skylight with my left hand. Maybe there was some way of breaking the window and climbing out. I thought of throwing the chair and then found a couple of house bricks in the corner of the room, but I didn't have the strength to throw them and my almost severed thumb prevented that kind of movement. I was getting weaker and yet my brain refused to channel that fact through to me. Still, in the tension of the moment, I did not realise the terrible extent of my injuries, but perhaps it was just as well . . .

I knew I had to stop the fire. I put the rag from the skylight to my mouth and nose to prevent further inhalation of the fumes. With my left hand I pulled at the blanket on the bed, trying to stifle the fire with it. I did not succeed. My strength had ebbed away. I pulled myself as far away as I could from the burning patch and watched the glowing light of the fire almost with fascination. I flinched: now that I was confronted with it, I feared burning alive. How could I have survived this physical attack only to die this way! It is probably one of the most painful ways of dying and I didn't want to have to suffer that as well. I hoped I would suffocate from the fumes before the fire got to me. I'd accepted that I had given up the struggle, as sounds around me took on an echo and the room's contents formed different shapes. I knew I was dying.

I was lying on the edge of the bed like a rag doll, waiting to die. How long I lay like that, I don't know, but it couldn't have been more than a minute or so before the door opened. I could not believe it. A man's voice drove into my semi-consciousness. 'The door's open,' it said.

My brain jumped and my body stiffened. Is he back? For a second or two I did nothing as I tried to digest what I had heard. Was it reality or a cruel deception, an hallucination? I could not quite puzzle out why the man didn't come in to help me. I tried to speak but nothing but a gurgling sound came out. I had no idea who this second man was. I stumbled to my feet and was aware of my movements being difficult to co-ordinate.

As I made it to the door I heard his footsteps running down the stairs. I leaned against the bannister and shouted out, 'Please help me, I'm going to pass out!' but the voice called back, 'Just keep coming down the stairs!' I was very weak by now but I knew I had to escape from that house to get help, get away from the fire and away from his shadow.

I didn't know how I was going to make it down the stairs. Walking down would be an impossibility. I slid to the floor on the top stair and, pulling against the bannister, bumped down on my bottom, leaving a trail of blood in my wake. Getting down all those stairs seemed to take for ever but at last I saw a shaft of light. I pulled myself to my feet. I knew I had to get down quicker. The thought of him springing out on to me from one of the closed doors filled me with terror. I could just see the front door. It was open and my freedom was just the other side of it. I tried to swallow but couldn't, and couldn't understand why. I felt the intense cold on my skin and a sharpening of the pain as the air reached the burns and the open wounds.

The last flight of stairs seemed the easiest – perhaps because I was spurred on by the sight of salvation. I pulled myself through discarded cartons and rags, rolling from side to side in the narrow passageway, my bare feet stubbing into boxes and debris. I had made it to the door.

Focusing was now more difficult after so much gloom, but I could distinguish the forms of people no more than twenty yards away waiting at a bus stop. There were at least half a dozen of these shapes and buses laden with passengers were passing by. I staggered to the top of the steps, held my arms out and screamed, 'Please help me. I've been raped!'

I swayed and leaned against the concrete pillar. The effort of getting that far had exhausted me. But no one responded! Here I was, naked on a cold February morning with my body covered in blood, too feeble to stand, yet they took no notice of me or of my pleas. They'd turned away. Hadn't they heard me? I tried to cry out again. My brain was urging me to scream, to shout, but I had no idea whether any sound was coming from my mouth. My mind was clear and alert and a crushing frustration overcame me. I knew I would have to get to the road, and sat down to gather my strength for the effort. I did not feel the iciness of the stone on my bare flesh. I couldn't swallow and put both my hands to my neck to ease the pain.

Everything was swimming around me and it was getting harder to breathe. I put my elbows on to my knees to give added support for my neck.

I don't know how long I was there like that. Time in these circumstances has no impact or importance. I looked up, responding to a dull noise, and could see only what appeared to be many little yellow hats running towards me from the other side of the railings that separated the road from the houses. An incredible surge went through me, tingling my bloodied, blue-cold body. 'I've been saved!' Relief swept through me. I wanted to laugh, to cry, to call out, to do anything to express my absolute joy, but nothing came out except, interminably, 'Thank you! Oh thank you!'

The unfolding scene was like a silent movie for, as I wavered between consciousness and unconsciousness, I heard practically no sounds whatsoever. No sirens from the fire engines, no noise from the pounding of feet or the unrolling of the fire hoses.

One of the firemen who was the first to reach me immediately noticed the blood pouring from the wounds at the back of my neck as I leaned forward cradling my neck in my hands. Then someone turned up the volume. He screamed for dressings. As I heard someone else approaching I lifted my head and removed my hands. 'We need more!' he yelled. My ears picked up the noise and intensity of the moment, yet it was like an echo in a drum. He hurriedly clamped his hands around my neck. I was, even then, still unaware that my neck had been slashed, let alone had bad it was. He didn't lessen his grip. I later learned that at first the firemen thought I had been a victim of an explosion, my injuries were so bad. The fireman who held my neck in a form of collar probably saved my life.

Now there were new faces around me — two policemen: a sergeant and a PC. They had come upon the scene in their patrol car after seeing the fire engine charging down the road — the road that was now almost blocked with rush-hour traffic. There was much talking and noise around me at the time. The hands clamped to my neck had not loosened and I was aware of concerned people trying to ease my cold and pain.

From somewhere I found the energy to speak and the words were actually getting out this time. The will was there to speak but the ability to do it was harder to find. I managed to tell them who I was and that I was on my way to work. I gave them the fullest description I could of my attacker, his colour, his hairstyle and a detailed description of his clothing. I was gently asked who I wanted notified. More than anything else I wanted my sister Sharon with me, for I knew she would look after things. I gave them her address but added that she had probably already left for work . . . but they didn't seem to hear the end. Someone was already off to make contact. I told them where I lived too and gave the address of my flat in Tulse Hill.

Someone called out twice, 'Where's the bloody ambulance?' It had been called more than twenty minutes earlier.

It's strange how the body and mind continue to feel and reason even when death is a few moments away. I was aware of sudden movement, of the urgency in the actions of those around me and of their faces full of concern. 'We can't wait any longer,' someone said, 'she won't make it.'

'Have to take her in the patrol car then,' said another voice. I felt hands lifting me gently and was aware that my feet were trailing on the ground. Someone opened the back door of the patrol car but I couldn't be pushed inside: if the fireman took his hand off the back of my neck the bleeding would start again. The door on the other side opened and I recall someone clambering on the back seat and stretching out towards me to ease me inside. Just at that moment an ambulance pulled up.

There was a sense of panic around me, and of voices raised in recrimination. 'Called you twenty-five minutes ago!' someone shouted.

'Had a computer breakdown – we've only known about this for five minutes!' snapped the reply. The PC kept talking to me, urging me to keep awake, to hold on.

I was lifted on to a stretcher, encased in a blanket and put on board the ambulance. An oxygen mask was clamped over my face and a drip was set up. I watched sleepily as its plastic container swung on its hook above my head. The ambulance set off for King's College Hospital in Denmark Hill, its siren blaring. A suction tube was slipped into my mouth to remove the blood and sputum accumulating there, but I wanted to spit it out, to get it away from me.

A policewoman was also on board with me and was sitting opposite, patiently yet obviously anxiously waiting for me to speak. Despite all I had just undergone, I felt embarrassed for her and for me that I had to spit. He had not totally robbed me of dignity then. Her questions came fast and were pressing and I responded as best I could. He was out there and must be caught. He could not be allowed to be free to do this again. That thought gave me the energy to speak to the policewoman as clearly as I could and to provide minute detail and description. Now, in retrospect, I don't know how I did it. As the ambulance had drawn away from the scene I took every opportunity I had to thank everyone, thank and thank them. Those words have never had such a sincere meaning as they did then.

As I lay in the ambulance I reflected, 'All those questions! The police aren't even waiting till I get to hospital.' There was a feeling of tired indignation. The sight of the alarmed faces of the firemen and the police officers flicked through my mind and I realised then that all the panic I had sensed among them was due to their wanting to help someone they believed was beyond help. They needed to get as much information as quickly as they possibly could from me; it really looked as if I would not make it. I signalled to the policewoman. I wanted to ask her if I would be OK, but just as I was about to, it seemed wrong and I held back. Of course I'm going to be OK, I told myself. I did pose a question though, one that, despite all I had endured, nonetheless frightened me in case I received a reply I didn't want. I asked if I had my rings on. I always wore three, of which two were particularly precious – my mother and father's wedding rings. Someone answered 'yes' to my query and I was calmed by that. But in fact only one remained. Gone was a silver ring of no real value, but gone too was my mother's wedding ring, the only thing I had of hers. The pain of its loss, when I eventually heard of it, made me feel as if I had been abused again, that he was out there, roaming free, and had taken something irreplaceable from me. I felt empty and sunken. I never even noticed that my knuckles had been deeply gouged when he had wrenched the rings from me.

By the time the ambulance drew up at Casualty it was estimated I had lost just over four pints of blood, half my body's blood supply, and my condition was critical. Neither the police nor the doctors were sure I would survive . . . but I was alive. I had made it – or at least as far as I was concerned!

As caring hands took me from the ambulance, I tried to re-orientate myself somehow, to grasp some sense of time. Fantastically, from the moment of his plea for help to the time I was comforted by the firemen only forty-five minutes had elapsed. Forty-five minutes that changed my life forever.

CHAPTER 2

Relationships

Being the youngest of four girls by seven years, I was completely indulged and spoilt rotten by everyone, with the possible exception of my sister Lesley. Up until my birth she had been the baby of the family and she admitted years later that I had 'stolen her sunshine'.

Sunshine is a good way of describing my childhood. My earliest memories are of laughter, happiness and love. Of course there were arguments. There were tears and various 'World War breakouts', but that's all very normal in a household of girls, three of whom were fast approaching adolescence. But if anyone was to harm or attempt to harm any one of us, we closed ranks and became a formidable force.

All four of us were born in London, just a stone's throw away from all our aunts, uncles and cousins. At this time my father was doing really well working for a vending machine company, so much so he was promoted to Area Sales Manager for the North West of England. So in 1966 we found ourselves moving lock, stock and barrel to the light industrial town of Bolton. I didn't know it at the time, but no one wanted to make the move. All our family and friends were in London, and Bolton seemed a very distant and mysterious place.

In those days the North/South financial divide was very marked, so, as unhappy as everyone felt about the move, we suddenly found ourselves moving from a small terraced house in a busy London street to a rather grand detached house with views in every direction over the most glorious and impressive-looking moors. It didn't take long to fall in love with the area. My sisters made new friends and Dad continued to work hard and impress his bosses. Only my mother was left out. Her brothers and sisters – she had six – and the friends she had known for years were all too far away to meet up with regularly, and she missed them passionately. As the demands of Dad's company grew, he was home less and less, so the girls, I in particular, became the sole focus of Mum's life. She lived for us.

Dad was becoming more and more confident in his entrepreneurial skills and, in 1972, he resigned from the vending machine company and set up in direct competition with it. Sadly his confidence was not matched by his ability, and the company could not sustain a large bad debt. He was declared bankrupt. We were going to have to tighten our belts and Mum, after a lapse of some fifteen years, was going to have to find herself a job. This she did relatively easily, but the stress and strain of the previous few months were too much for her and, on her very first day at work, she suffered a massive heart attack and was dead before the ambulance reached the hospital. She was only fifty years old.

I was nine then but I miss her still with an intensity that the passing years have done little to diminish; except for the time I spent at school, we were together for every second of the day. Wherever she went, I went. I was her shadow from the day I was born to the day that she died. Her death left a huge sadness in my life, but I came to understand, even then, that hard knocks only make me stronger and more resilient.

Shortly after the funeral our house was sold and the proceeds from its sale were used to pay off some of my father's creditors. We moved to a very small two-up, two-down terraced house in a part of town where the toilets were still in the back yard. The front room of our house was a sweet shop, and Dad did everything he could to earn a living from it, but he eventually turned his talents to the building trade. It was a sad time in all our lives and it made me grow up very quickly. Within months my sisters had all left home: Loraine, the eldest, married and rented a flat near our old house; Sharon took a year off after her A-levels and went to France to work as an au pair; Lesley decided to travel around the world. I wasn't the baby of the family any more, and nothing would ever be the same again.

My father was not the world's best businessman, but he became the world's best dad in my eyes. Before Mum's death, he had always been away, but now he was there for me. He encouraged me in everything I did, especially in sport – his all-consuming passion. In his heyday Dad was one of the country's finest hockey players. He represented England many times, and only missed playing in the 1956 Olympic Games because he was threatened with losing his job if he took the time off. Of all his girls, I was the only one to inherit his huge enthusiasm for sport. From the age of ten I was in the women's Rounders League, and I played tennis and netball at competitive level. My number one sport, though, was badminton; as a junior I represented Greater Manchester.

Dad remarried when I was fourteen. I had known my stepmother, Myra, for some time and had grown to love her. I welcomed her into our family, and likewise she has treated me as a daughter. She was an only child, and had never been married before, so taking on our family must have been quite a daunting task.

Mum's premature death precipitated many things in my sisters' lives. They are all career women now, but if you were to ask them what they were planning to do when they were at school, you might be surprised to learn that marriage, husbands and babies were very high on their agendas.

Loraine has brought up her son Daniel single-handedly, juggling child-minders, school schedules and business commitments to become Commercial Director of a vending machine company in Warrington. Her son, following in Dad's footsteps, is a gifted hockey player, having represented Lancashire for the past four years and the North West of England for two.

Sharon, however, became my role model. She was everything I wanted to be: successful in her chosen career and financially independent. She became a Board Director of a major London advertising agency before she was thirty, met her husband-to-be, John, as a student, and now has three wonderful young children, Merlyn, Jennifer and Richard.

My relationship with Lesley was quite different. I had usurped her position by being born, and she wanted nothing to do with me. I, on the other hand, longed for her attention. When Mum died, Lesley started travelling, finally putting roots down in Spain where she and her boyfriend Pat own a large apartment. Every morning she crosses the border into Gibraltar to her office where she is now Head of Trust & Company Secretarial Department for the largest law firm on the Rock.

With all of my sisters involved in hard-nosed commercial business, how did I end up in fashion design? In truth I had only ever wanted to be a PE teacher, but throughout my childhood, and mainly due to lack of funds, I designed and made all my own clothes, and then began to do the same for my friends.

Fashion seemed to be a more exciting, though not necessarily well-paid, option. So, at the eleventh hour, I changed my mind and opted for a BA Honours degree in Fashion for Textiles at Brighton University. I became a fresher in 1985.

Being a student at Brighton was an education in itself. It was so totally different from Bolton: cosmopolitan, creative, individual, diverse, classical and modern. For me it had the buzz of London and the calm of the East Sussex countryside. I found the mixture intoxicating. In a way, it gave me permission to be as outwardly flamboyant as I already felt inside. But Brighton was an expensive place and my grant only just covered the basics. To make ends meet I had to get an evening job, and so for three of my four years at Brighton I worked as a waitress in various restaurants and wine bars in the town centre. That way I was always certain of having a decent meal too.

The friendships that I formed in my first year at University are a major part of my life now. They are my second family. Tony, Chip and I were on the same course, and got on well from the very start, so it wasn't long before we were renting a flat together. In this group too – and, incidentally, nearly always in the flat – were Heather, Chip's girlfriend, and Chantelle. Together we would manage to balance the heavy workload and the heavy social life to make the best use of our time at Brighton. We all loved soul music and dancing; it was the perfect release after a long week at College. A club near the seafront, the Brighton Belle, offered both and it was here that I met two fourth-year students, Sue and Sakina, who were to become my close friends too. When Sakina was producing her final collection, she asked me to be her first-year helper. From that time a special bond developed between us that has grown stronger over the years.

I don't believe that lasting friendships just happen; they have to be worked at, nurtured. I think I have unconsciously done this for most of my life. 'The family' is very important to me. This could be directly related to the loss of Mum and the fact that I still feel robbed of the love and affection of one of the most important people in my life. It could be that I associate the happiest of times with family life and want to continue to replicate them. Either way it matters to me that I feel very much part of the family.

When I graduated in July 1989, I was employed by the Conran Design Group. It was here that I met Valerie, also a newly recruited graduate, from Ravensbourn College. When we met there was an instant rapport. She became my best friend, my surrogate sister. People would often mistake us for sisters. Her family became my family, and mine hers. However, within three months the Conran Design Group had been broken up by its parent company, Storehouse. I found myself in the design studio at Bhs, and Valerie was at Richards. Now that we were no longer seeing each other at Conran every day, we had to work harder at meeting and, wherever we could, juggled our European and US schedules to do just that. I still saw all my other friends at weekends, and Valerie always spent Friday through to Monday in Bournemouth at her boyfriend's, but our relationship was special, and was to prove exceptional in the tragic months that were to follow.

This chapter would not be complete without a special mention of New York. In my third year at University I was lucky enough to be sent there as part of my year out in industry. I was working for an international textiles company called Westwood, and there got my first taste of the vast differences in the American and British approaches to the fashion industry. For a start, everything moves faster in the States, decisions are made more quickly and designers are immediately respected for their talent and expertise. Annoyingly, American fashion houses prefer to employ British fashion graduates because our training and standards are regarded as superior.

Westwood was based in the garment district in Manhattan. I shared a flat with my friend Sharon in Brooklyn, so I had to walk through areas that were not particularly salubrious. However, I never once felt intimidated by my environment. I was never bothered by anyone in the six months I was there, nor on my subsequent visits.

Through Sharon I met Ali; both were ex-Brighton students. Ali had been nicknamed Brighton's patron saint of New York. He took me under his wing, and looked after me like a big brother during my six-month placement there.

I loved New York and, thanks to Sharon and Ali, felt at home immediately. It was a dynamic city to work and live in. Many of my friends had secured top-flight positions within design companies after graduation, and that was exactly what I wanted to be part of. This dream was never realised. At the age of fifty-eight my dad suffered a heart attack and died. I was just weeks away from my finals. I couldn't believe that he too had been taken from me. Since Mum's death I had had eleven years of his undivided attention and now, apart from the happiest of memories, my only memento would be his wedding ring, which I had altered to fit my finger, just as I had done with Mum's all those years earlier.

CHAPTER 3

Casualty and the Hospital

My sister Sharon received a phone call at her office from the au pair. The police had been to the house. She immediately rang the nanny to check on her daughter, Merlyn, and then she rang John. Finding that the problem wasn't there she rang BhS to check on me. They told her that I hadn't turned up for my early morning meeting. My sister was puzzled as she knew how important this meeting was, and it was now nearly 9.30 a.m. Just as she was putting the phone down, a police car drew up outside and two officers entered the building. Sharon was beckoned over and approached them apprenhensively, thinking, 'What could I possibly have done to warrant two police officers?' These policemen had been with me on the doorstep. They both seemed to be suffering from shock and as a result were less than clear in describing what had happened to me. At first they said that I had been mugged, abducted off the street more than two hours earlier and knifed. Then they told Sharon that I had been raped. They seemed unsure whether the attack had been made by one or two men and more importantly they could not say if I was going to survive. It was only in the car on the way to the hospital that she learned of the fire too, when the policeman said that I might have been affected by smoke inhalation . . .

I was rushed from the ambulance into Casualty. Two blood transfusion lines were run immediately into my arm and my lacerated hand was bandaged tightly. One of the Casualty doctors, Ruth Brown, spoke gently, explaining that I needed to have some X-rays taken.

'Where's my sister?' I asked.

'She will be here soon,' Dr Brown whispered.

Sandbag-type blocks were put around my head to prevent movement while I waited for a brain scan. There were quite a few people in the scan room when I was wheeled in. One woman was very gentle and motherly. I held her hand tightly. I couldn't focus very well but I could hear a younger woman speaking over me as if I was not conscious or able to understand. She jerked her head towards me: 'Every time I see something like this, I want to know what happened.' It seemed to me that it was certainly not an expression of concern, but of a desire to know all the grisly details. Given the state that I was in and all that I had endured, it is interesting that I could still find it possible to be disgusted.

The X-rays were crucial. Without them the operation that was urgently needed could not take place. The procedure was excruciatingly painful for me as my head was held and turned first this way, then that, pulling on the open gashes. I called for something to drink, for the constant thirst was agony. Nothing to eat or drink, I was told, until the surgeons had made their decision.

Once the X-rays had been completed, I was taken back to my cubicle in Casualty. The curtains were pulled aside and a man entered. He introduced himself as the police forensic examiner. He stood erect and aloof, the epitome of professional rectitude. I instinctively felt that he had no sympathy for, nor even under-standing of, my feelings and fears; what I had endured meant nothing – it was all in a day's work. I shivered. In a soft voice he told me what had to be done. Swabs were to be taken from my mouth and vagina. He had to take a blood sample too. At this time I was numb. I had started out that morning with such high hopes and enthusiasm. Here I was, only one hundred min-utes later, having my body probed in the most intimate way for a report. Even in my weakened state I knew that this was nec-essary, but it did not lessen the feeling of being dehumanised again. The examination was probably made worse because it was carried out by a man who I felt was cold and impersonal. I cannot believe that a woman examiner would have been as dis-tant as he was, and a woman would certainly have been easier for me to accept under the circumstances.

When Sharon arrived at Casualty I was still in X-ray having the brain scan. All she wanted to know, in her anxiety, was when she could get to see me and be with me. She needed to feel assured that I was all right. She was met by Dr Ruth Brown and shown into a pleasant room with very comfortable furniture, pictures hanging on the walls and a bowl of flowers standing on the small table. Everything had been designed to be as agreeable as possible for people in distress. A tray of hot tea and a plate of biscuits were immediately brought in and my sister was shown the telephone and told that it was at her disposal.

However, telephoning was not on Sharon's mind. She made only two calls, one to her bank manager to see that my cheques and credit cards were stopped, and one to her husband. He couldn't be located so she had to leave a message. Sharon was agitated and would remain that way until she saw me. If she had telephoned any of the family then, what could she have said? She could only transmit her own turmoil without being able to answer any of the questions that would be bound to come. The waiting must have seemed interminable to her. I was back in Casualty. 'Just a little longer' and Sharon could see me: there was someone else with me just then. At last she was taken through to my cubicle just as the forensic examiner was leaving.

'Have you got everything?' she asked him.

'Yes,' he replied with a fixed grin.

Sharon had been my mother figure since Mum died. She had had shock upon shock that morning but nothing could prepare her for the one she now had as she came through the curtains in Casualty. Even I could see how she reeled from the sight. I had no idea how I looked. I was thinking as normal, so why should I look any different? My wounds were open and livid and weeping. The trachea was exposed. My body was blue and swollen by numerous cuts, grazes and bruises. But the most fearsome of all was my head and face. The flesh above my collarbone had swollen greatly and taken on a mauve tint. My eyes were protruding from their sockets and had an eerie glutinous luminescence about them. (I was later to learn that the effect on my eyes was typical of strangulation.)

'Nice waistcoat you're wearing,' I croaked. It was mine, one that I had made in fact.

Sharon burst into a grin of relief. Her first impression had been that I was blind. All the blood vessels in my eyes had burst, leaving piercing green irises. Obviously from my comment I could see and I was lucid. She leaned over me and kissed my forehead and clutched my left hand. She was teary and trembling slightly. I ached to tell her that I was OK.

We chatted quite normally about so many things. I asked about the important meeting she had had the day before. This reassured her that I was coherent. I wanted so much to reassure her. I learned later that I had whispered to her, 'He didn't penetrate me, didn't penetrate,' yet I do not recall it. They were words that I would not think of using. I can only guess that it was the terminology used by the policewoman questioning me in the ambulance. I was subsequently told that I had not been raped in the legal sense. I had his semen in my body, but because it was not vaginal 'penetration', it was not considered to be rape.

A photographer came into the cubicle. I was uneasy with having photographs taken but I thought they would be necessary for the police. Little did I know that the photographer was from the hospital and his work would be invalid in court. The police photographer never got the graphic pictures of my open wounds because he did not turn up until the next day, by which time my wounds had been treated. The hospital photographer had been with me about five minutes when Dr Brown came in with a kidney bowl and a syringe. She was to take a blood sample for the forensic examiner. But I told her the man had already taken some. This turned out to be only half correct. He had made five attempts at taking blood from my groin, none of which was successful. Dr Brown did it in one.

I didn't want to be alone. I wanted to talk. I felt this would keep people with me, around me, and I needed that more than anything; but my *ability* to talk was poor. Swallowing was a near impossibility. I was reliant on the small suction tube that had been placed in my mouth since the ambulance ride. I asked Sharon to make some phone calls. The first was to my work, to explain why I had not turned up. I hated to think that they could believe that I would just let them down. Also I was meant to go to the theatre that evening and my friends needed to be forewarned too. Maybe they could get someone to go in my place. It never dawned on me how they would all be affected by what had happened. And I wanted Sharon to speak to my best friend, Valerie. She was very close to me, just like a part of the family, but I wasn't ready to see her yet, not at this stage.

Unbeknown to me, my sister did not make any of these calls until much later. Being with me mattered. Everything else could wait. Sharon stayed there holding my hand and, as frequently as she could, asking the nurses for a drink for me. The thirst was a strange and odd pain and one of the hardest to endure at that moment.

We were interrupted by a bustling that started on the other side of the curtains. A man was screaming loudly, a piercing scream filled with pain. He had been stabbed in the groin and was bleeding profusely. The sound of his cries chilled me and filled me with fear. This was the second potentially lethal assault in the area before noon that day – that we were aware of. There was nowhere to put him, so my stretcher was shunted from the cubicle into the corridor to accommodate him. This totally dismayed my sister, who asked about the room that was due to be allocated to me. She wanted to know what was happening about my unattended wounds and whether I could have something to ease my constant pain, and reiterated her plea for me to have a sip of water. I had by now been without liquid intake since 6.45 a.m. when I had raced through my flat with a cup of coffee, leaving half of it because of the rush I was in.

My sister's persistence paid off. She was given a couple of ice cubes. She gently rubbed one over my lips. Ah! At last . . .

Time dragged on . . . waiting, waiting. It was now well after two o'clock and I was still on a trolley in the corridor; still naked. My only cover was a tin foil blanket, which is designed to give maximum heat and protection against shock. I was shivering constantly. Sharon called for blankets and two were wrapped round me. I began to feel a tingle of pleasant warmth but my feet were still freezing. My sister was about to take her tights off to wrap round them when a nurse suggested bandaging them. It was only then that Sharon discovered the black marks on my legs and feet: burn marks.

It was six and a half hours before I was wheeled from the corridor and given a room to myself in the Panta Rialla ward. It took several nurses to lift me off the stretcher and into the bed. They were trying to protect my injuries but the ache throughout my body was indescribable and the pounding in my head was so intense. Painkillers were still not allowed. Just as the bed manoeuvre was completed my brother-in-law John arrived. The police had managed to track him down and break the news. He's always hated hospitals, but he stood at the end of the bed, clearly distressed. I remember asking him if he was OK and if he would like a cup of tea – the great British solution. It was very comforting to have Sharon and John with me. It was at this point that I realised that I needed the ones I loved to be nearby. I asked Sharon to speak to my best friend again and tell her that I had changed my mind and that I wanted to see her.

Several doctors came in shortly afterwards. They examined me over and over again. They seemed mostly preoccupied with the swelling in my throat and how to anaesthetise me suitably, still allowing me to breathe. A tracheotomy was the obvious solution, but, as most of the lacerations were in that area, they opted for a tube through my nose and throat. The doctors were all associated with the plastic surgery department. Dr Graham Buckley operated on my neck, Dr Manuel Oyarzabal on my face and another surgeon, whose name I never learned, was to operate on my partially severed thumb.

Outside, in the corridor, Sharon was aware of a woman looking her way as if unsure whether to approach her or not.

Eventually she came across. She asked Sharon if she was a relative of Merlyn Nuttall, then introduced herself as WPC Nicola (Nicky) Holding. She had been assigned by Brixton police station to be my liaison officer. I developed an instant liking for Nicky, who eased my next few days, in fact my next year, considerably. Nicky came from Brixton's Rape Squad Investigation Team. She had been told of the sexual attack but was totally unprepared for seeing my injuries. Although she regained her composure quickly, she had visibly paled. She asked me a few questions to verify the description of my attacker that I had given earlier and left with a fairly good idea of what had happened. Her visit was brief. Once outside my room she fainted!

A nurse arrived to prepare me for the operation. I stopped her cleaning my hands. 'Nothing has been taken from under my fingernails yet,' I told her. I had watched *Quincy* on TV. It was normal police practice to take samples in such cases. After all, there was a high chance that I could have scratched him during our violent struggle and have his skin under my nails. Nicky was contacted and she called the forensic examiner back to the hospital to finish his job properly. He arrived at five-thirty that afternoon and was clearly not happy about it.

He asked my sister and brother-in-law to leave the room and laid a small sampling set out on the bedside cabinet. Without a word he snatched at my injured right hand and dug deeply under the broken nails for the matter that had clogged there. I felt a jolt of pain sear through my hand and I let out a stifled scream. Sharon and Dr Oyarzabal ran back into the room but Sharon was told to withdraw. His grip relaxed but he continued roughly to cut my nails to the quicks and store them in a container. Maybe I was being super-sensitive but that was no one else's impression. It seemed obvious to me that he was upset at having to come back to the hospital for what should have been routine. Whatever it was, my hand and fingers throbbed for hours after that.

It was with a mixture of relief and apprehension that I was wheeled down to the operating theatre. Sharon held my hand as far as she was allowed, assuring me that everything was going to be just fine. The pre-med felt wonderful. It cleared my nose momentarily. Then I felt the tube being inserted, pushed up my nose and into my throat. This made me want to gag . . . then I heard the anaesthetist say his usual, 'I am going to count,' but before he had started I was out. I was on the operating table for just over two and a half hours. The surgeons worked wonders neatening the jagged edges of skin around my neck. Three hundred internal stitches and one hundred external stitches chequered my throat and the back of my neck. There were a further twenty stitches pulling my thumb into place.

News of what had happened travelled fast via the media, although those close to me were unaware that the victim they were hearing about was me.

Sharon had had to leave a message for my best friend Valerie. It was 4 p.m. before she found out what had happened. She did not want to hear any details over the phone, but offered to ring round all of my friends and break the news. They were all stunned, some more so because they had been following the news reports on the radio all day and had been commenting on how horrific the attack was. We all read the headlines every day: another girl raped; another murdered. We have all become accustomed to such news and very little shocks us any more, because of course it never happens to anyone that we know. This time it had.

Valerie left work at 5 p.m. and drove straight to King's College Hospital, trying desperately not to look at the headlines on the newspaper stands. She did catch sight of one under

Waterloo Bridge that made her blood run cold: 'Rape Victim Has Neck Slashed and Survives'. When she arrived in the ward there was just Sharon and John sitting in my empty room. She felt a flash of panic, but in fact I had gone down to the operating theatre.

There was no point in anyone staying at the hospital while I was being operated on. Besides, my sister had to face the awful phone calls that she had been putting off all day – telling our family. Thank God that Daddy was not alive to hear this news. He was so protective of all his girls. This he would not have been able to bear.

The hospital rang Sharon and Valerie at nine o'clock as I came out of theatre. Nobody thought that I would be awake and even if I was, they predicted it would not be long before I dropped off to sleep again. This just did not happen. As the anaesthetic wore off I became as alert as ever. Was this due to the nervous system still fighting for life? A feeling of warmth and happiness overwhelmed me. It was so good to have a drink, and for the pain to have eased. It was so good to be alive!

Sharon had explained to Valerie what had happened, more or less, but in her distress she had not told her how I looked. As soon as Valerie received the phone call from the hospital she set out on her way to see me. She bounced into my room totally unprepared for the sight and stopped in her tracks. I did not look anything like her best friend. We both said 'Hi!' and she gently sat on the edge of my bed. It took a few minutes of chatter before she accepted that I was 'still the same old Merlyn'.

I really wanted to speak to my family and friends. I wanted to tell all the people I love that I had survived. At the time it did not dawn on me that perhaps another reason for wanting to talk to them all was to convince myself that I was safe now. A telephone could not be connected in my room. However, Dr Oyarzabal, arranged for me to be pushed, bed, drips and all, to the recreation room where there was a payphone. Valerie did all the work; she held the receiver to my ear, dialled the numbers and put the money in. 'Surprise' is an understatement for all the people I spoke to; they were picturing me at death's door and here I was waking them up in the middle of the night and speaking quite clearly. I remember being totally amazed at everyone's reaction. The enormity of what I had been through really had not sunk in. I could not believe that my sister was coming all the way from Spain. I could not believe that none of my friends had been to the theatre.

Valerie was a tower of strength. She realised that I was desperately tired, but I was fighting sleep. The thought of sleep somehow made me feel that I would be vulnerable again. We talked throughout the night and she tended my every need. I had asked Sharon for a mirror earlier, but she had been insistent that I should not find one. I tried again with Valerie. She got a mirror from a nurse and gave it to me. I looked into the glass . . . and looked. The image I saw was ugly; horrific. How could I look like that when I felt so together, so normal? I knew I had had stitches, but I did not expect to see so many, or the red, bulbous eyes. There was so much disfigurement. My head was so *big*. I was speechless.

I finally dropped to sleep from exhaustion. Valerie slept curled up at the end of my bed. Sharon arrived at the hospital at around six o'clock the next morning and headed straight for my room. Before she came in she composed herself, but she was in for another shock. My head had swollen to almost double the size overnight and I looked much worse than I had before going into surgery. She burst into tears when she saw me. So did I. It was the first time that I had cried and I did not even know why

I was crying: perhaps it was from the combined tension and exhaustion, or perhaps it was just because I was reacting to Sharon's feelings.

At about 8 a.m. three student nurses knocked politely on my door. They asked if they could come in and see me. All three were black. One of them instinctively held my hand and they too burst into tears. They said that they lived in the Brixton community and walked the same route as I had, every day. They kept repeating how desperately sorry they were. It was very strange; three complete strangers standing in front of me and apologising for someone they did not know. I reassured them that I felt no hatred and that I was fine, but I was puzzled at how they knew where I had been walking.

I did not realise that news of the attack was already widespread. Tabloids and broadsheets all reported it, from the *Daily Star* under 'Fiend Slits Girl's Throat', through to *The Times*: 'Sex Attack. Woman's Throat Cut'. *Today* had 'Thug Leaves Victim to Die', the *Daily Mail* went with 'Knife Man Slits Girl's Throat in Sex Attack', and there was a major item in the *Daily Express*. I was not to see any of this until much later: all reports were studiously kept away from me.

My liaison officer, Nicky, had told me that I would have to give a statement. I just wanted it over and done with. I felt it was like a weight hanging over me. She arrived later that day with another WPC. Despite my heavily bandaged right hand, I managed to hold a pen and draw a rough outline of the layout of the room where I had been attacked. (Later I was asked to sign this sketch as it turned out to be so accurate. It also testified to the state of my memory.) Nicky took out her pad and asked me to go over the whole affair again. Sharon stayed with me throughout this additional ordeal, but this time I had to go over and over every movement and every thought, the angle, the timing. I had told Nicky the whole story the day before but she wanted more, much more this time. Fixing my concentration was hard and my head still ached but I was determined to get this over and put it behind me. Although the will was there, fatigue finally took over and I had to agree to continue the next day.

The police required every small detail of the sex attack, but I found it difficult to put into words. Yet, while feeling this way, I also knew that if I didn't give the police everything I could remember, I would be depriving them of their best chance of catching the man who had put me through this ordeal. How many steps did I take to the grass verge at the front of the house? What was his exact position in relation to me? What were his expressions? What were his movements like? Exactly and precisely what did he do to me and how did I react to his swings of mood? It was important that I recollect any tattoo or significant mark on his body. Was he on drugs, what did he take and how? I answered all the questions as best I could. I surprised myself at the amount of detail that I could recall, but I could not picture his face. No matter how hard I tried the only feature that I had embedded in my memory was his big, staring, protruding eyes.

Every page had to be signed, any changes had to be initialled. And it was all to continue the next day . . . When Nicky left I felt both relieved and frightened. I knew that I would not be able to sleep without being haunted by images. I would probe my mind for his face, another feature, the order that things happened in. The thought process was exhausting. Little did I know that this was the very beginning.

My close family and friends travelled from near and far to be with me on the second day. Their mere presence was a great source of comfort. By now I was acutely aware of how I looked and I tried my best to put my visitors at ease. I was becoming accustomed to seeing people peering through the door so they could compose themselves before entering. Everyone seemed to be going to great lengths not to distress or upset me, but the funny thing was that I was probably in much better shape than all of them. I had accepted what had happened and was simply rejoicing in the fact that I was still alive to see all my loved ones.

From the beginning of day two I was getting a steady stream of flowers and gifts. The policemen who had been with me on the doorstep, and then brought my sister to the hospital, came to the ward early. One of them, PC Simon Carroll, stood self-consciously in my doorway holding the largest bunch of flowers I had ever seen.

The other officer, Sergeant Simon Seeley, handed me a card and told me that the words inside were very sincere. I was so touched by their concern and I must say a little puzzled. Surely the police saw crimes of this sort every day. Wasn't it all in a day's work? No, apparently even for them it was not. Every Brixton police officer seemed to feel responsible in some way. This had happened on their patch and they assured me that my attacker would be found. Their words gave me hope, but I knew it wasn't going to be easy.

Within the next few days the switchboard was to be inundated with calls asking after my progress. I received over fifty bouquets and countless cards and messages of goodwill. I could not believe the number of people from my past who had put pen to paper when they heard what had happened: old friends from school, their parents, members of my old sports clubs. This one attack affected so many people; there was a ripple effect of emotions. My other two sisters and my stepmother had now arrived. They had all taken the news badly, but were totally calm and collected by the time they came to the hospital. In fact when Loraine arrived she took on the persona of 'Miss Efficient'. The hospital administrator had complained to Sharon that the ward's telephone lines were being clogged up with calls for me and could she get a mobile phone. Just like that. How many people can just get a mobile phone and have it immediately connected? Loraine did. One call to BT and within an hour my new lifeline was installed. Little did I know that in the future my 'moby' and I would become inseparable . . .

The hospital staff were very good to me throughout my stay and did not impose any restrictions on visitors. That factor was a major contributor to the speed of my recuperation. I have always been at my happiest when I am surrounded by my friends and I needed that now, more than ever. I felt so loved. Just one glance around my room confirmed that cards, presents and flowers filled every square inch. Every day, and particularly every evening, until late at night, it was party time. Friends and family alike arrived with bottles of champagne. The corks popped and the laughter was contagious. I could neither drink nor laugh much, but I thrived on the atmosphere. It was the only time when I felt comfortable enough to sleep, hearing the sound of everyone enjoying themselves. The nurses seemed fascinated by the endless stream of fashionable people coming and going. It was something new, lively and optimistic.

For me it was a kind of celebration. I had survived the whole ordeal and my attacker had not deprived me of the will to live, or the right to live life to the full.

One thing struck me as the days went by: men and women reacted totally differently to the attack. All the men, from the firemen and police to my own friends and relatives, had shown anger. They wanted blood, they wanted revenge. Most seemed to feel ashamed for what had been done to me by another 'man'.

They felt diminished by his deed and frustrated that he might never be caught to pay for his crime. Their tension and concern was real and very tangible. The women surrounding me took a totally different attitude and were only concerned with me and how I was coping. They were carers and did not have time to address their feelings for my attacker yet.

I was unaware that I might need any sort of protection in hospital. It had not dawned on me that it might even be necessary. I enjoyed my daily walks around the ward. All the other patients had now got used to how I looked and were very grateful for my overflow of flowers. It seemed that I lifted their spirits. I felt safe being on my own in hospital. This was until I discovered that the newspapers had printed my exact location. The police were disconcerted, and my family were frantic. I found out by accident when hospital security came by to discuss my request for a guard on my door. Of course it was a request that my sisters had made. I did not know that ever since my sister Lesley had arrived from Spain, she and Valerie had taken it in turns to sleep across my door at night. They wedged a rolled-up magazine through the door handles to stop anyone entering unannounced.

From this point my independence had gone. I could no longer walk to the toilet on my own, let alone visit my new friends in the ward. I felt a panic reaction. He had tried to kill me once. Why wouldn't he want to finish the job? I was well aware that he was capable of murder. I no longer felt safe. I asked if I could leave the hospital as soon as it was physically possible. Just six days after I had been admitted, I left.

CHAPTER 4

The Reconstruction

I was so relieved to be going home – home being Sharon and John's townhouse in Camden. He couldn't find me there, could he? He did have the entire contents of my handbag, but he would never find the Camden address. It had been in my Filofax which, although badly fire-damaged, was now with the police undergoing forensic tests.

My mind was working overtime, and this communicated itself to everyone around me, so much so that when one of my sisters saw a male nurse, who just happened to be black, who just happened to have a flat top hairstyle and who just happened to be approaching my room, she flung herself against the doors to bar his entry. He carried on, obliviously, until he caught up with the doctor he was following, barely glancing at this crazy woman, looking for all the world like a demented starfish!

Physically leaving hospital would be no mean feat. I had been given so many presents, so many personal mementoes, sent so many flowers and so many cards, it would take the best part of a day to pack. I phoned Sharon and John. They were already on their way to collect me. They were going to have a long wait, though, because Nicky had just arrived. She told me that the police artist was coming to see me. I would have to help him draw a likeness of the man who had tried to kill me. No, she didn't know exactly when he was turning up and yes, the work had to be done at the hospital. Today. All the sketches would then be printed overnight in time for the police reconstruction scheduled for the next morning.

The police artist was practically bent double under the weight of all the books and materials he had to carry, but I soon realised why it was necessary. I must have looked through hundreds of pages of face shapes, noses, eyes, ears, hairlines, trying to build up an image that I, and hopefully others, would recognise. This was something I had tried to do ever since the morning of the attack. I had searched and searched my memory but could only recall his big, wild eyes. The truth is that I never really got a good look at his face in the first place.

I'm sure there must be hundreds of people out there who cannot understand this. How can you endure a sustained, violent sexual attack over a forty-five minute period, without seeing your attacker's face? Without having it etched in your memory for ever? Impossible? Well, actually it's really easy. You are so terrified you become numb. You are so frightened you can hardly think straight. You are told not to look at his face. You follow instructions. To the letter.

Because of this, arriving at a likeness that was as accurate as possible was a lengthy process. One area I felt more confident about was his clothing. Although I'd been unable to look at his face, I'd had ample opportunity to look at his tracksuit. I had given an exceptionally detailed description of it to the police while I was still sitting on the steps of the squat in Brixton waiting for the ambulance. Now I did the same with the police artist: satin-finish nylon tracksuit in dark blue, white and yellow; zip from yoke to neck; light panel across the chest carrying the hummel logo. Unfortunately I was unable to see the finished visual because the police artist had to get back to the station to prepare the handouts. And by now I was shattered. I just wanted to go home.

A police reconstruction is a re-enactment of the events leading up to a crime, usually an extremely violent one, and is carried out at the precise time and in the precise location where the actual crime was committed. People who bear a good resemblance to the victim and attacker(s) are enlisted to assist; the same or similar clothing and accessories are sought and the media are called in to lend their help reporting it and televising it.

The only difficulty here was that on that day I was wearing clothes that were not readily available in this country. Sourcing the items was going to be tricky: my Chanel silk scarf was a fake bought in Japan, my chiffon pleated palazzo pants came from Paris, my jacket was an original – mine – that I had handwoven and made myself, and I had designed and made my overcoat. The only three belongings that were relatively easy to duplicate were my shoulder bag, my desk Filofax and my Shelly shoes. So, on my third day in hospital, amidst the chaos of innumerable visitors coming and going, statements being made, examinations being carried out and medications being administered, I set about organising the 'props' for the reconstruction, enlisting the help of Valerie, my nearest and dearest friend.

Within a couple of days all the clothing and accessories had been assembled, and Valerie had agreed to be 'me' in the reconstruction. Because we were such close friends we knew this was going to be a traumatic event for both of us. Just how much we wouldn't know till later. However, that was a whole day away, and I still had to leave the hospital.

By the time the police artist had left, it was dark. It was only about 5 p.m. but this was February. I have always been an extremely confident and outgoing person, but right then I felt very, very vulnerable. An incident had occurred that morning which, on top of everything else, had given a huge blow to my self-esteem. There was a new nurse on duty, or at least she had not been there for the past six days. She was a vast black lady, the sort you just knew would be full of fun, and could cheer you up instantly. As I passed by she took a long look at me and exclaimed, 'My God, what a frightening sight you are!' I tried, despite my shock, to make light of it and said she should have seen me before, to which she replied, 'I can't believe you looked any worse!' I knew I must have looked pretty hideous, but until then not one person had shown the slightest revulsion at my appearance; nervousness, yes, apprehension, certainly, but this reaction was so totally unexpected, particularly coming from someone who was surely used to seeing some gruesome sights. She made me feel embarrassed and ashamed of myself, emotions I had not felt since the attack took place. I felt like a circus freak. It was sad too, because up until that moment, with the exception of the woman in X-ray, I had nothing but admiration for the professionalism, commitment and spirit of the King's College Hospital staff. It's strange that it should be two women who ended up offending me.

Sharon and John had been waiting patiently outside my room for three hours while the police artist and I worked together. Occasionally they had to turn people away, including a physio-therapist, so the work could continue uninterrupted. (The physiotherapist said she would return before I left, but never did.) They now packed all my things – I could give very little help as I could hardly move my head and neck, and my right hand was out of commission – and loaded up the car. Hours earlier I had been ready to go, but now the thought of going outside made me feel incredibly nervous. Just leaving the hospital ward took all my courage; everything suddenly seemed so hostile, and I was aware that everyone was looking at me. Worse, not looking, but staring. Now I know how a road traffic accident victim feels as the cars slow down and their occupants drink in every gory and ghoulish detail. I did my best to disguise it, but I felt total panic.

Once inside the car I felt slightly safer, but the journey across London took a long time as we had set off right at the peak of the rush hour. When we parked outside the house I could see a large banner greeting me with 'Welcome Home Aunty Merl'. It brought an immediate smile to my face. Loraine was inside with her fourteen-year-old son, Daniel, and Sharon's daughter Merlyn. I am godmother to both of them and was anxious about how they were going to react to seeing me in my current state. Merlyn had obviously been told that I had not been very well and could sense the upset, but I knew she had missed me. I badly wanted to cuddle my little niece. I wanted to nuzzle her baby-sweet-smelling neck and feel her tiny arms around mine. The feeling was so strong I almost ached. She was only two now, but I had been present at her birth and had seen her practically every day since. She meant everything to me.

Daniel was always extremely sensitive and impressionable, and it distressed me to think he might be aware of any of the details of my attack. Unfortunately the newspapers had provided him with quite vivid and lurid descriptions.

I had deliberately worn a scarf around my neck to camouflage the wounds, and a pair of unseasonal sunglasses to hide my eyes. The thought of frightening the children, or even being rejected by them, made me feel physically sick. I needn't have worried. As soon as I entered the hallway both Daniel and Merlyn rushed over to me and swamped me in hugs and kisses. I explained that I had hurt my neck before taking off my coat and, eventually, my scarf. Danny seemed to take it all in his stride. Little Merlyn became instinctively protective, holding her small hand to my neck, saying to everyone, 'Don't touch my Merlyn, sore neck.'

How normal this all seemed. I had been given a mug of tea, *Coronation Street* was just starting and Merlyn was sitting on my lap. In fact the only sign of the devastation in my life was the stack of newspaper cuttings piled up in the corner. For a brief moment I felt safe and blissfully happy. I had somehow managed to cheat death. Sharon was still arranging some of the flowers that had arrived at the hospital for me, and as I looked at them I realised that but for my physical strength, and a huge dose of luck, those flowers could so easily have been for my funeral.

Six-thirty, Tuesday morning, 25 February. It was a dull, slightly misty morning in Brixton. Even at this time the traffic was starting to build up and the area was full of people standing about and waiting for something to happen. They were mostly uniformed and non-uniformed police officers and a few journalists. The once-grand Victorian houses looked at odds with the modern vista of shops, but one house in particular was sending shivers down Sharon's spine. She and John had gone to the police reconstruction as moral support for Valerie, who was playing the starring role in a sordid and disgusting episode of real life. None of them knew what the house on Effra Road really looked like, apart from the description I had given. In the gloom of this February morning, an insignificant, down-at-heel squat had a forbidding and sinister presence.

I watched all of this on television, holding Loraine's hand tightly all the while. I was hoping that the reconstruction would have the same effect on me as it was intended to have on passers-by: I'd remember some vital clue that was locked away in my subconscious. That never happened. My recall directly after the event was crystal clear.

Valerie began her journey at the exact time and place I had begun mine one week earlier. She looked just like me, right down to the hairstyle. It was impressive, but she must have been going through hell at that moment. She was preceded by a phalanx of the press corps, and an army of police officers followed, enthusiastically questioning every single person they came across. They handed out leaflets with my attacker's likeness together with a detailed description and illustration of the clothes he was wearing that day. As Valerie approached the side road, the precise point of my abduction, my stomach was in a knot. He was going to appear. He was going to subject me to all those horrific acts again. And then, without any prior warning, this tiny man appeared and marched Valerie off towards the squat. He must have been at least six inches shorter than her and, to be quite frank, if it hadn't been for the importance of the occasion, I would have giggled at its apparent absurdity. I later learned that the man playing my attacker was in fact a policeman, but he was the only black officer living nearby who sported a flat top hairstyle.

When Sharon and John returned they had brought back copies of the hand-outs for me. At first I thought I was mistaken, but then I realised that, despite all my statements and descriptions, which had never changed from the first day, the police had 'rearranged' the pattern on the tracksuit. The tracksuit described in the police hand-out did not belong to the man who attacked me. I had been so precise at all times and now I felt that the investigation would be placed in jeopardy over this one small detail.

How do you judge the success of a reconstruction? By the amount of media coverage achieved? The number of people questioned? The number of enquiries received? All I know for sure is that this particular reconstruction was mounted with extreme passion and professionalism, but it did not deliver one positive lead.

I was finding it difficult dealing with the here and now. The media had taken this news item to their hearts and there was substantial and continuing coverage. The police were confident that they were near to making an arrest. However, seven days after the attack no arrests had been made, no charges brought, and I felt as though I was treading water, just waiting for him to find me and finish the job. After all, I was the only witness to this crime; I was the only one who could point the finger at him – or so I thought.

Lesley wanted me to go and stay with her in Spain, but I felt reluctant to leave in case there were any developments in the investigation. Then, not long after, my girlfriend Chantelle rang. She was disturbed because she had received an anonymous phone call in the early hours of that morning. She knew that I kept all my friends' phone numbers on a card in my purse, and my attacker would therefore have easy access to it when he stole my shoulder bag. Call it paranoia, call it overreacting, but I made up my mind there and then that I was off to Spain where I would be unknown, and could start to relax a little. Removing myself from the goldfish bowl I was in at the moment could only be good for me.

*

Before I could leave there were a number of things I had to do. First I needed to see my sister's GP to be given the 'all clear' to leave the country. Sharon had already taken so much time off work she was unable to come with me and, as there was no way I was able to go anywhere on my own, my girlfriend Sakina accompanied me. My sister had already explained the reason for my visit, so I was ushered by the doctor's wife straight into the surgery. There a truly comic scenario was enacted. At the sight of me, the doctor gave me the impression of being plunged into a state of shock. Far from his being able to help me, it was me who did all the talking, me who had to administer tender loving care to him! The physical examination of my neck and hand was conducted at a distance of around one and a half metres. He wouldn't, or couldn't, touch me. After I had asked his advice about the healing properties of aloe vera and vitamin E creams, he spent the rest of the time fumbling through a directory, clearly more at ease with it than with me. The consultation didn't last more than ten minutes and no further treatment was discussed or recommended. Sakina and I had to rush from the surgery before our stifled sniggers erupted into gales of laughter.

What a preposterous situation to find myself in, I thought, yet I was beginning to feel that this was probably the norm. How would other victims of violent crime cope in the same circumstances, especially the ones without a large network of family and friends willing to lend support? What about those who perhaps weren't articulate enough or weren't able to see or talk to anyone? What about those whose confidence and self-esteem had hit rock bottom? Who would help them?

'Counselling' appears to be the panacea for today. It is the first and last word in coming to terms with anything and everything. Well, I didn't want counselling; I didn't feel I needed counselling, but, as everyone kept going on at me, I gave in and agreed to see the counselling assessor that Bhs had arranged for me. The idea was that on my return to the country a specific psychiatric counsellor would be assigned to me.

One aspect of my experience, which has run like a recurrent theme from the day of my attack to the present, is that while I have coped with my personal tragedy through the joy of having survived it, most of the people I have met are unable to deal with what happened to me, and that includes the very people who have been there specifically to help me: doctors, surgeons, police officers. More importantly, those closest to me seem unable to understand my own reaction to it. Shouldn't I be a gibbering wreck? When am I going to break down? Conversely, I have had relatives say to me, 'Well, I suppose you're over the worst now, aren't you?' The truth is you can never 'get over' something like this. Ever. You just adjust to the fact that it has happened, and try the best way you can to live your life on your terms – not on anybody else's. I have tried many times to analyse why I feel so strong, and have come to the conclusion that I, unlike many other victims of violent crime, have never felt (or been made to feel) the slightest bit of guilt. I am convinced, too, that my positive mental state enabled me to heal physically very quickly. The fact that I thought I was going to die on that day has changed my whole outlook on life. Far from feeling embittered and angry about what happened to me, I treat each day as a bonus.

My penultimate task before leaving for Spain was to revisit King's College Hospital to have the stitches removed from my hand. Being right-handed I was naturally concerned about its lack of mobility, but I was worried too about the wounds to my neck. I had assumed that, given time, the mobility would return and that the NHS would help in reducing the scar tissue that was rapidly forming on my neck. The stitches were removed painlessly, but the doctor didn't mention whether or not I would need any physiotherapy, and I didn't think to ask. Going back to the hospital on that day was an unpleasant experience; I had to travel through parts of south London that now only held dread for me. I had to wait my turn in a crowded Casualty, all the time feeling that 'he' was just around the corner, waiting to silence me.

Finally I had to move all my things out of my beloved flat in Tulse Hill. Chip, Heather and John took me there, because I wanted to supervise the removal, but it was probably a bad idea because I was continually fatigued. I was finding it impossible to sleep at night, partly because I was still in some pain from my injuries and the surgery, but mainly because with the night came the silence. Then there was more time to think, to brood, and with the darkness came a deeper sense of vulnerability. I was on my own. As in hospital I really only felt comfortable drifting off to sleep during the day surrounded by family and friends.

While everyone was packing cases and boxes, I went into the bathroom to do the same. There I noticed the skylight window was open, but as I went to close it, I froze. This was the skylight in that squalid little room in Brixton; this was the skylight that I couldn't open; this was the skylight that was my only means of escape, the difference between life and death. I managed to call out feebly to John, and he took me away. I had been forewarned to expect many more flashbacks like this one, but from that day to this there has not been one.

I left the country the very next day, precisely two weeks after the attack took place, and I didn't know when I was coming back. As long as he was at large, I felt I wasn't safe in England.

What I didn't know was that just one day after the attack, during the media furore surrounding it, a slightly built blonde girl – she couldn't have been more than twenty-four or twenty-five – stood nervously outside Brixton police station. She didn't like the police, but she didn't like what had happened to me either. At the back of her mind there was a question she needed an answer to. Depending on the answer, she would know for sure whether or not she was living with a deranged rapist and potential murderer. She waited until she could see that the front office was clear, then walked quickly towards the duty officer – she certainly didn't want to be seen going in or out of any police station. In a low, barely audible voice, but without any prevarication, she asked him a particularly blunt question relating to my assault, wanting to know whether a specific sex act had been carried out on me. The duty officer asked her to wait while he fetched someone who could help her. When he returned, she had gone. She hadn't given her name or address, so there was no way of contacting her. No one at Brixton thought any more of it at the time, but it was to be of crucial importance in the coming months.

CHAPTER 5

'The Sheltering Shame of Brixton'

The headline in the *Caribbean & Asian Times* screamed 'Mean Streets That Can Make A Victim of Your Sister . . .' The article was about the attack on me one week earlier, but here I was being described as 'a sister' and 'of African descent'. When I queried this with the police press office, I was completely amazed to discover that this misinformation had been circulated to the black press deliberately. 'We always get a better response from the community when they think it's one of their own,' an officer told me. I couldn't work out why this was thought sensible, given that the nation's media, from the tabloids to *News At Ten*, were also covering the story at the same time, and it was quite clear that I was not black!

Was this the jaundiced view of a police force who felt the community was against them and everything they stood for, or was it an isolated response from a tired police officer? Either way I felt deeply shocked to learn that the colour of my skin could affect people's perception of the nature of the crime and their willingness to help in solving it. But why did I feel shocked?

This was merely racism in reverse; there would be a lot more black people than white who knew exactly how I felt just then.

Any police investigation relies heavily on the support it gets from its local community and from the media too. It was not difficult to get media coverage and support due to the severity of the assault. However, I found it hard to come to terms with the lack of any information, let alone hard evidence, emanating from the Brixton community.

It was bad enough that I was abducted off a busy main road in broad daylight, in front of a bus stop full of people, and no one appeared to notice. It was bad enough that, forty-five minutes later, naked, having lost four pints of blood in a frenzied attack, I screamed at passers-by to help me, and was completely ignored. The only person who actually came to my aid was an illegal African immigrant, Henry Olusegun, who was squatting in the house in Effra Road. It was Olusegun who opened the door to the smoke-filled room I was locked in, and it was Olusegun who called the fire brigade. No one else lifted a finger to help. It was as though I didn't exist. I was subsequently told by a friend – in all seriousness – that I should have shouted 'fire', because I would have had a more positive response!

Afterwards, following all the news reports pleading for information, people seemed more willing to come forward. After the reconstruction the police were inundated with calls. Local shopkeepers were only too happy to be able to help by displaying the 'wanted' poster on their premises. Even those who had been deliberately avoided because of their known hostility to the police telephoned the station asking for copies of the poster to display. For a while I truly believed that my ordeal had drawn the police and the Brixton community closer together. The majority of people had been genuinely upset by the brutality of the assault and they were trying to be helpful, but not one of the people who responded really knew anything. Yet there were people who did know quite a lot, but they never came forward of their own volition.

What made the community feel so unable to commit itself to helping the police find my attacker, to put him away before he did this to someone else, someone who might not have been as lucky as me? The journalist Peter McKay wrote a no-holds-barred account for the *Evening Standard* one month after the attack, where he questioned the meaning of the phrase 'the community', where this kind of outrage can go unpunished for so long. He called it 'The Sheltering Shame of Brixton':

. . . This week's *Crimewatch* on BBC1 is to broadcast an appeal for information on the 18 February Brixton case in which a 27-year-old woman was kidnapped at knife-point, sexually assaulted, choked with cheesewire and left to die in an attic room which the attacker had set fire to.

Somehow, slashed to ribbons and having lost four pints of blood, 'Sarah' escaped and has since had to endure painful medical treatment, including 200 stitches.

Isn't it sad that, one month on, no one has come forward with hard information on this case? It isn't an ordinary everyday assault. This is crazed savagery. The person who did this should never see daylight again. Someone must know him. Someone must have identified him from the photofit pictures. Someone must have decided to let him stay at large. As 'Sarah' says: 'Someone knows something. They have to ring the police.'

We often hear about 'the community' and 'community leaders' – usually in connection with interested parties seeking money or control of the police. Huge amounts of money are squandered by these communities in make-work schemes, leisure centres and other civic absurdities with the express intention of buying votes. But, what has the community done to find the fiend who attacked 'Sarah'?

Looking at the photograph of 'Sarah' yesterday, her once-pretty face a mass of scars, reading of her suffering, you wondered what kind of 'community' shelters someone capable of this.

Yet the police were so appalled by what had happened to me, they even had a whip-round to buy replacements for my personal belongings that had either been taken or destroyed during the attack and the subsequent fire. They went to the most extraordinary lengths to find out exactly what I needed without arousing my suspicions. Not only did they telephone Sharon and Valerie for hints, they would discuss the matter internally! 'Is it Clinique skincare products she uses?' one officer shouted over to another at Brixton police station. 'What colour Filofax would she like to have?' another officer appealed to his colleague over the police radio. I had never really had any dealings with the police before but, I have to confess, I felt a far greater sense of 'community spirit' with the police than with the people of Brixton. I knew that they cared and, strangely, I almost felt they were on a crusade to catch my attacker.

I have never thought there was anything remotely glamorous about police work. To me it appeared a rather dull, demanding job with more troughs than peaks, more down sides than up. Through working closely with the police I gained a new respect for them, for their total dedication to finding whoever was responsible for the attack, for their sheer doggedness in the face of insurmountable odds and for their tact, understanding and sensitivity when dealing with me. These were qualities I never expected to find in such plentiful supply. I also gained a much deeper understanding of the vital role they play in our community.

For many people who live outside London, Brixton conjures

up a picture of racial tension and unrest; of black versus white; of drugs-related violence. Memories of the riots in 1985 are hard to erase and, with the riots following the death of Wayne Douglas in police custody in 1995, it is difficult to see how the police and the Brixton community can ever be reconciled.

But is Brixton really a bubbling cauldron of violence, more so than any other inner-city area? If you compare the Home Office criminal statistics for England and Wales and the Brixton Division crime statistics, the all-encompassing 'Violence Against A Person' offence increased by nineteen per cent over the past five years (1990–1994) in the United Kingdom. In Brixton the increase was only nine per cent. What is perhaps more shocking is that figures just published on violent crime in the year to June 1996 show an overall increase of ten per cent, the largest increase for eight years.

In 1991 'Operation Dalehouse' was established. This was a Metropolitan Police initiative to counter the increasing violence resulting from trafficking in crack and crack-cocaine. Much of this violence was attributed to a particularly powerful group of criminals from the West Indian community: the Yardies. What separated them from the rest of the criminal element in Brixton and South London was the extreme punishment they would mete out to anyone who opposed them, threatened them, or generally tried to cash in on their 'business'. And, when they needed to, they could disappear amongst the large West Indian population and be indistinguishable from their God-fearing, law-abiding 'brothers'.

The Yardies liked to convey an image of power. Carrying a gun was normal dress code and the bigger the gun, the greater the power. Their adolescent, machismo-imbued approach to life – and this did not change with the onset of years – manifested itself in their abysmal treatment of their women, their constant quest for status and their total disregard for human life.

(Was I attacked by a Yardie? The police were almost certain that he must have been stoned. His mood swings during the attack were consistent with the effects of taking crack-cocaine. Yet this wasn't a tit-for-tat crime.)

Then there was a small core of people who were so suspicious of the police they would not speak to them, however evil and depraved the crime. Small wonder then that no one came forward with information to help the police investigation in my case – yet this core was the group most likely to know what had happened on 18 February 1992, why, and who was responsible.

These were not the images I had in my head when, in October 1991, I decided to move from my rented room in North London to a rented maisonette in Tulse Hill, a residential area just a few minutes' walk away from the heart of Brixton. Even then the area was 'up and coming', going through a process of gentrification. Designers, artists and media people were forsaking the more pretentious (and far more expensive) areas of Fulham and Putney to set up home here.

As most of my friends lived in South London, I used to pass through Brixton quite regularly. While I was only too aware of inner-city crime, I had always been very careful as far as my own personal safety was concerned. In other words I considered myself to be as streetwise as the next person. My impression of Brixton as an area was one of energy, vibrant colour and laughter. Once I had moved near there I felt at home in the community even though I wasn't a local. I now shudder every time I hear its name.

On the tenth day after the attack, and after seeing the police reconstruction, one person came forward with something concrete to offer. Mr Gall, a delivery driver for a bakery, had parked his van just outside the side entrance to the houses on Effra Road. He'd been up for the best part of Tuesday morning already, and it was only 7.15 a.m. He was very tired, but something made him glance up towards the parade of Victorian houses, where he saw a white woman and a black man standing close together. The man was holding her right arm, and they appeared to be quarrelling. The baker assumed they were having a 'lovers' tiff'. He thought no more about it until he received a police hand-out with details about the attack and a description of my attacker.

On the same day at 2 p.m. Sean Cremin, a twenty-four-year-old cab driver with Knight's Hill Radio Cars, a local firm based in West Norwood, South London, was just finishing his shift. He was glad it was over, as the traffic seemed unusually heavy now, and he wouldn't have to deal with it for the rest of the day. That's why he liked the early shifts: no traffic, no hassle. He'd had quite a busy morning, and should have felt pleased with himself. Instead he was feeling angry because one of his passengers had 'done a runner'. This had more or less obliterated his profit.

He reached out to turn his car radio off when the first news reports of my attack began to filter through. As he listened he thought back to one of his fares that morning. He had picked up a passenger at a flat in West Norwood at 6.20 a.m., and was told to go to an address in Effra Road. When he was halfway there, the passenger, a young West Indian man, told Cremin to stop at a well-known spot for buying and selling drugs. When he eventually arrived at his destination in Effra Road, the young man told the driver he had to go and get the money for the fare from a friend inside. He walked between the iron railings that separated a row of large Victorian houses from the main road, and disappeared inside one of them. After about ten minutes the cab driver realised he wasn't going to see his money, and there was no way he was going into that house to try and take it. He turned his car round and headed back to base. It was 6.50 a.m.

Sean was still sitting in his car, locked in thought, when his boss shouted, 'Haven't you got a home to go to?'

Sean looked up, startled, and then realised where he was. Smiling he replied, 'On way.' He flicked the car radio off as he said to himself, 'This has absolutely nothing to do with me. Nothing. I'm not getting involved.'

CHAPTER 6

The Investigation

It was a busy Saturday morning in Streatham High Road on 29 February 1992. Opposite the Leeds Building Society stood a tall, slim man. He was in his mid- to late-twenties and was sporting the flat top hairstyle that was so popular then. He looked calm, but his jaw and mouth were rigid with tension; his clenched fists were thrust deep down into the pockets of his bomber jacket. He was not going to make his move until there were fewer people inside. Then, as a couple left, he saw his chance and sprinted across the road. He shoved open the heavy glass door of the building society and walked straight up to Marian John, the cashier, who also happened to be the Branch Assistant Manager, and said, 'You made a mistake, I gave you two cheques with a total value of eighty quid, and you've only put in fifty. Sort it now!' He didn't so much speak as snarl. The woman stepped back a little, taken aback by his threatening behaviour. She didn't know who he was, let alone why he should be so aggressive towards her, but she wasn't going to take any chances.

'I'm sorry, but I'm unaware of the problem. Could you wait here while I call the Manager?' She forced a smile as she said this, but her hands were shaking as she reached for the internal telephone. There was something about his eyes that she found very unsettling.

The Manager, David Duggan, was there within seconds. He had already heard the commotion from his office. 'Good morning, Mr, er, Ferrira,' he said, craning his neck to see the name on the pass book. 'I'm the Manager, Dave Duggan. How can I help?' As he did this, he surreptitiously pressed a security button that operated the overhead CCTV camera. This procedure was always adopted if any of the staff thought someone was behaving suspiciously or becoming violent.

As it happened Ferrira was right. The building society had made a mistake. Someone had inadvertently keyed '£50.00' into Ferrira's pass book when the value of the cheques had been £80.00. The manager rectified the situation and Ferrira left, but not before fixing the cashier with a look. She remembered thinking to herself, 'That's one guy I really wouldn't want to meet on a dark night.'

The original transaction had taken place on Tuesday, 18 February 1992, at ten o'clock, approximately two hours after I had finally struggled to the bottom of the stairs of that miserable house in Effra Road.

It was around this time too that the police investigation swung into action.

It is very hard to 'commit the perfect crime' because there is always someone who notices something. It may be the smallest, unconnected detail, but in the hands of the investigating team it can become a crucial part of the jigsaw which makes all the other pieces fall into place.

So, how do the police tackle a case of this sort? First, a senior investigating officer is put in charge. They are appointed on a rota versus workload basis. I have to say that I consider myself fortunate to have had Detective Chief Superintendent John Jones handling my case. The first thing I was told about him was that he had never failed to get a conviction. It may sound silly, but right there and then it was very reassuring to me. The first thing he did was to set up an Incident Room. An Incident Room is usually only set up to investigate murder cases and violent series crime, such as a serial rapist, but due to the extreme brutality of my assailant, John Jones was going to make an exception. He, like everybody else, was confident of bringing the perpetrator to justice.

Just talking to John gave me confidence and hope. He had vision and the ability to see the bigger picture. He was a strategist and a leader, and he inspired others. He never gave the kind of knee-jerk reaction lesser men succumbed to in order to satisfy an over-excited public or a baying press. The stereotypical, narrow-minded, bigoted policeman was anathema to him. Although he was a very busy man, he spent a lot of time with me. He kept me up to date with developments. And, most importantly, like Nicky, he treated me as an equal, without patronising me, and without treating me like a china doll.

While John Jones would be responsible for the overall running of the case, he would also be involved in a number of other serious crimes, so Detective Inspector Hamish Brown was appointed to handle the day-to-day running of the investigation.

One immediate difference between this kind of investigation and a more 'normal' police investigation lies in the number of officers devoted to it on a twenty-four-hour basis. In this case there were fourteen in total. They were taken off their normal duties and drafted from other stations. The only other difference between this Incident Room and others was that due to the number of murder cases already being investigated at that time in South London, computers would not be available. All the information would have to be compiled and filed manually.

Of all the officers involved in this ten-month-long investigation, inevitably I would get to know some better than others. There were officers who were outstandingly committed and courageous; there were officers who said one thing and did the opposite; and then there were others who would tell me exactly what I wanted to hear, even if it was untrue, to make sure I would give evidence in court when the time came. They all had one thing in common, though: everyone worked like Trojans to find my attacker, and, when he was eventually sentenced, no group of people could have been more elated, with the possible exception of my family.

As my liaison officer, WPC Nicola Holding represented the police and their continuing investigation when she was with me, and represented my point of view when she was with the police; or at least that was my interpretation of her role. She was in constant contact with me from the day of my attack until weeks after the trial at the Old Bailey. She had guts, determination and persistence, and she had an innate sense of right and wrong, all of which invited praise from some quarters and criticism from others. She became one of the family and I trusted her completely. My attachment to her was not a gradual process; from the very first day that she appeared in the hospital, only hours after the attack, I instinctively felt that this was someone who could empathise with me. And I was right. To say she was special is to understate her contribution. She was one in a million.

Detective Constable Mark Chapman was in charge of all the exhibits in the case. It was his job to process and categorise all the evidence. He had to keep track of every fingerprint, every fibre, every speck of blood, every DNA sample, every state-ment. But he was also one of the first officers on the scene that Tuesday morning, and saw for himself the impact of the attack on me. He was able to secure and preserve the crime scene, which was difficult given the extensive nature of the house and the condition it was in post-fire fighters. That action was to pay dividends later on in the investigation. But he did more than that. As time went on and the police seemed no nearer to catch-ing my attacker, Chapman and Holding joined forces, eventually working on the case in their spare time.

Finding evidence, then weaving together disparate pieces of it to tell a complete and coherent story, is what good police work is all about. Without it a motive cannot be established; without it a case cannot be built; without it a villain cannot be caught and kept off the streets. Well, evidence we had in plenty: 150 separate exhibits, as the police call them. Of these, sixty-five were sent for DNA testing, and of the sixty-five, eight were sent for PCR testing (a different kind of DNA analysis).

The one thing I have learned when it comes to evidence is that it is not the quantity that counts, it's the quality. And the best way to get rid of evidence is to set fire to it. What the fire doesn't destroy, the fire fighters do – under gallons of water.

Collecting evidence from the house in Effra Road was a dirty job. This house was well known as a squat, but it was also known to police as a place where crackheads would go to do drugs. It was owned by Lambeth Council, and its longest stand-ing lodger was a black woman called Maureen Barnes, otherwise known as Slings. She rented the top two floors of the four-storey house, which included the attic room where I was assaulted. She would often let friends use that room to smoke crack. However, Slings had decided to leave the Brixton area. She had moved during the night of Monday, 17 February. Before going, she had swept all the common parts and put the rubbish into bin liners.

It was difficult to establish just how many people were in the house at the time of my attack and, with the exception of Henry Olusegun, no one ever came forward.

When the Scenes Of Crime Officers (SOCO) arrived at the house, much of the evidence they had to deal with was smoke-damaged, burned or waterlogged, or all three in some cases. They dusted for fingerprints where they could, and the rest they bagged up for further forensic examination, including one length of bannister, which had to be sawn out.

The police were confident, and I was convinced, that this evidence, together with the swabs and fingernails taken from me at the hospital, would lead to the identification and arrest of my attacker.

These days DNA testing or 'genetic fingerprinting' has gained wide acceptance as the most infallible method of police detection. DNA or deoxyribonucleic acid is the master molecule of life. It carries the coded messages of heredity, which govern everything from eye colour to allergies, and it is present in the cells of every living creature. When DNA is extracted from a specimen of blood or semen and dosed with a radioactive probe, it will expose a piece of photographic film. The resulting pattern of stripes is a DNA 'fingerprint'. In theory no two people can have the same fingerprint. So, if my attacker had left any traces blood, hair or semen on me, the police would have water-tight evidence with which to convict him. Or so I thought. After what seemed like ten months, but was in reality ten weeks, I was informed that it had been impossible to get a clear reading from the semen sample taken from my throat. It was decided that a different form of DNA testing would be conducted: Polymerase Chain Reaction, or PCR, an amplification technique. PCR, while not as conclusive as genetic finger-printing, is especially useful where the sample for examination is minuscule and/or the quality of the sample is too poor. The bonus is that PCR yields results in a fraction of the time.

It's sad but true that I have been so conditioned by television that I had expected results to come back if not by the end of the first day then certainly within two. In the real world it just doesn't happen that fast. First of all there were, and still are, a limited number of laboratories available to handle this kind of analysis. To conduct PCR analysis at that time, there was only one laboratory in the UK, located in Chepstow, Gwent. The scientists there were only taking on a small amount of serious crime work. Our evidence had to join the back of the queue and, as all the cases were of a serious nature, it was impossible to queue-jump. The whole process was time-consuming, with forensic results merely dribbling in to the police. With 150 separate exhibits to handle it's not really surprising that the pace seemed a little on the slow side. But being logical wasn't helpful to me. I was impatient and had assumed that everybody wanted to catch my attacker as much, and as fast, as I did. I also knew that any delay gave him a greater opportunity to cover his tracks and to leave the country – or to remove me.

After another three weeks I was told that the PCR process had also failed to deliver any worthwhile results. I couldn't believe there was nothing. I felt fobbed off with the reasons I was given: 'It's because he's a drug addict . . . the quality of his semen is too poor.'

'What about my fingernails?' I asked. 'I had a violent fight for my life with this man. Surely you've got something from that?'

'No, nothing, I'm sorry.'

My frustration and distress were, unfortunately for Nicky,

aimed at her, the bearer of bad news. I believed that somewhere amongst all the forensic evidence would be our trump card in the investigation; I had therefore asked to be given dates by when certain results would be ready. I attached enormous importance to these dates and, when no one called me, I would ring the police station and make a nuisance of myself. I wanted and needed to know what was going on. And so far there wasn't even inconclusive evidence, let alone the conclusive sort! How could this miracle of twentieth-century detection fail me? Who ever heard of DNA testing not working? But maybe it hadn't failed and somehow the raw evidence had become contaminated. Could it be human error? I wondered. I knew that the forensic medical examiner had found traces of semen in me, and there must have been traces of flesh under my fingernails too. But I also felt that he had been extremely sloppy and unprofessional at the hospital, which led me to believe he was at fault, rather than a proven scientific procedure that can provide reams of information about a person just from the examination of an isolated hair follicle.

Someone was given the job of finding a duplicate of the hummel tracksuit. Hummel already manufactured the tracksuit and strip for Tottenham Hotspur Football Club, and I had assumed that there was only one design. Wrong. There was a multitude of different hummel tracksuits, each one slightly different, but none of them was exactly as I had described it. Then there were the counterfeit ones to consider. It might have been one of those, in which case it would be virtually impossible to find the distributors and retail outlets. The police could leave no stone unturned, so manufacturers and wholesalers were contacted, both here and abroad. However, despite all the efforts a duplicate tracksuit was never found.

Four weeks after the attack the only things the police knew

for certain were that my attacker was black, had a flat top hairstyle and was wearing a hummel tracksuit – and I'd told them that much minutes after the attack.

It was time to leave. I was off to sunny Spain and I was petrified. Flying was something I used to do all the time when the fashion shows were on. I never gave it a second thought. But now I was thinking of nothing else. How was I going to cope in the airport with all those people around me? On the plane it was bound to be worse, because I couldn't get away if he was there. On the outside I might have looked in control, but on the inside it was controlled chaos. I needed to go to feel safe, but I didn't know how I was going to get there because I was too frightened to travel! Simon Gregory came up with the solution.

Simon is an ex-boyfriend and we have known each other since school days. He has always been regarded as one of the family, and is the one person that I think knows me better than I know myself. At that time he was working in the Marketing Department at British Midland, and he not only arranged for me to have a free flight to Spain but also said that he would be my personal bodyguard on the flight. I felt much better about travelling under these conditions, but I was still on my guard throughout the whole trip. From Malaga Airport Simon drove me in a hire car to my sister's house in Algeciras in Southern Spain. Not until we were there could I relax. I would stay there to recuperate and until I felt it was safe to return, in other words, when *he* was behind bars. The whole family felt that this was the best thing. Best for me, because since I had left the hospital there were round-the-clock visitors to Sharon's house and I was not getting any rest – I actually didn't mind this at all, but I knew I needed more rest if I was to recover properly; best for Sharon and John, because they were both back at work but were only getting as little rest as I was; best for little Merlyn, because the continual interruptions meant she could not sleep – and it would be a whole year before her sleeping routine returned to anything that resembled a normal one.

The one thing I hadn't bargained for in leaving the country was a feeling of disconnection. What had kept me going over the past fortnight was the frenzy of police activity: constant updates, constant questions. Now it had virtually stopped. Everything was to be filtered through Sharon and not me, because I wasn't so accessible in Spain. I felt out of it, cut off. I needed to feel involved at all times!

Just before I left for Spain, the momentum of the investigation had noticeably slowed. I had agreed with John Jones that I would give an exclusive interview to the *Sunday Mirror*, and had granted permission for one of the more gruesome hospital photographs to be shown in the same article. The aims in making the details of the attack public again were, hopefully, to regenerate awareness, interest and ultimately leads for the investigation. The article appeared, and it created an impact as far as the callousness of the crime was concerned, but no leads.

Shortly after I arrived in Spain, I did get one phone call from the police which brightened my day. *Crimewatch UK* had agreed, after a degree of coercion from the Brixton Press Office, to run a feature on the attack on their BBC1 television programme in mid-March. This was brilliant news as the programme always appeared to get results. None of us knew exactly what they were going to do, but whatever they did it would, at the very least, be a great memory jogger.

On the night of the programme all my friends and family were waiting, fingers poised on the 'record' button in case someone missed it. My sister Lesley tuned in to the British Forces television channel in Gibraltar so that I could see it live. Police from the team were at the television studio and manning the phones in the Incident Room back at Brixton. The programme started and we waited and waited; then, towards the end, a very short piece was transmitted about the Brixton case. A snippet from the police reconstruction video was used and the poster was shown; and that was it! A bank robbery warranted more time and was, therefore, seemingly more important on the day. Twenty-five calls were made to the studio offering information; ten to the Incident Room. Not one of the callers gave a real lead, and not one person mentioned my attacker's name. I felt let down, disappointed and sorry for myself. After four weeks it seemed that everyone had forgotten all about the attack. I was old news.

What I hadn't realised was that *Crimewatch*, at that time, never showed a reconstruction of a major crime like this unless the crime was six months old. So just showing a snippet after four weeks was actually quite a coup. If I had known all this prior to the transmission of the programme, I would not have felt so dejected, but no one had prepared me.

At a council flat in Streatham Hill a young couple had settled down for the evening. They too were watching *Crimewatch*. When the report on the Brixton attack was broadcast the man leaned forward to get a closer look at the face on the 'wanted' poster. His girlfriend, Jeanette, didn't appear to be paying too much attention to the programme and, after a while, went out to make some coffee. Long after the programme ended, he was still staring at the television screen.

'Are you all right?' Jeanette asked. 'You don't look too good.'

'I think I've just seen myself on TV,' he said, but he sounded dazed. He got up and headed for the bathroom. He closed the door behind him, took a couple of sleeping pills from the bottle in the wall cabinet and washed them down with some water. He carried on doing this until he had swallowed over twenty-five sleeping pills. He slowly but deliberately went to the bedroom and lay down on top of the bedcovers. He felt pleasantly light-headed at first, then a little drowsy, then nothing. What seemed like moments later he could hear a muffled commotion; then people shouting; a woman crying; now a cool breeze was rustling around his head and body; now someone was pulling at his face and mouth. He wanted them to stop but he couldn't open his eyes. Suddenly he was gagging; something was being pushed down his throat. He had to make it stop. He tried to use his hands to take the obstruction out of his mouth, but it was impossible.

Jeanette had found Tony fast asleep on the bed but thought nothing of it. It was only when she went to the bathroom that she saw the open bottle of sleeping pills, her sleeping pills, and there were none left. She flew to the bedroom to try and wake him up, but it was useless. She rang for an ambulance, and one was there within five minutes.

The Casualty doctor wanted Tony to stay in for observation, or at least until he had his strength back, but his patient was unwilling to comply. The doctor thought of trying to persuade him again, but the look in Tony's eyes told him he'd be wasting his time.

From the moment he left the hospital, Tony's personality changed. He refused to go out; he wouldn't see any of his friends, and he wouldn't even sleep in the flat any more. Instead he took a sleeping bag on to the roof every night and slept there. (This went on for seven days.) Jeanette knew there was no point in asking him why he was behaving like this. From experience, she knew he would say it wasn't her place to question him.

Jeanette wasn't stupid. She'd recognised all the signs weeks ago. He was hiding something, and it was something big. Even though she'd had her suspicions, she didn't want to believe they could be true. After his suicide attempt and his self-imposed 'house arrest', she was certain: he must be responsible for raping and cutting that girl in Brixton a few weeks ago. She realised she couldn't keep this information to herself. She knew how violent he could be, especially to women; she'd suffered herself enough times. She also knew how differently he behaved under the influence of drugs, especially crack and crack-cocaine. And she knew about his sexual proclivities. She'd endured so much from him herself, but she couldn't allow him to get away with such an horrific crime. What if he did it again? What if he did it to her?

A couple of days later, Tony kissed her goodnight and took his sleeping bag on to the roof. Jeanette waited for five or six minutes, to be sure that he wasn't coming back, then picked up the telephone receiver and dialled the number of Brixton police station.

You could practically feel the collective sigh of relief go round the Incident Room. At last, a real lead. For the past five weeks the whole team had been following up flakey leads, taking statements, visiting likely suspects, taking blood samples from known users of the house in Effra Road – Tony had been identified as a user, had been contacted to come forward to give a blood sample, but had not yet done so – but no progress was being made. Now came this gift!

Tony's full name was Anthony Ferrira. His nickname, however, was Ripper, and he was a very, very dangerous man. He was twenty-seven years old and had spent most of his adult life in prison. From the age of sixteen years he averaged three convictions a year: assault, robbery and possession of offensive weapons and drugs was the usual combination. In 1981 the nature of his crimes changed, and he was arrested and convicted of sexually assaulting a thirteen-year-old girl. Four years later, while in prison, Ferrira got into a fight with another inmate, and killed him by stabbing him in the chest and head with a pair of scissors.

On 26 March at around 5 a.m., four unmarked police cars drove into the car park behind the flats at Streatham Hill. Eight police officers headed quietly towards number 16. On the word from DI Brown one of the officers broke open the front door, and the rest 'steamed' in, making safe each room until they located the bedroom. Ferrira and Jeanette were woken from a sound sleep. (It was important that Jeanette looked surprised, because everyone knew that if he suspected her of being the informant he could harm her from any prison he was in.) As Ferrira was dragged naked from his bed, DI Brown read him his rights. He was given some clothes to put on and driven straight to Brixton police station for questioning. It seems curious that such a 'hard man' went so quietly and without fuss – almost as if he had expected the police to call.

The police then began a painstaking search of the flat. They were obviously hoping to find clues that would link Ferrira to the attack. Specifically they were looking for my handbag, which had not been found amongst the debris, my Shelly shoes that he had so admired, his tracksuit, which would be saturated with my blood, and Mummy's ring. It was almost a pleasure to search this flat, if searching a flat could ever be called a pleasure. It was exceptionally clean and tidy. Everything was in its place and, despite the small dimensions of this home, there was a place for everything. The wardrobes were a revelation: every shirt was ironed and hung on a hanger, every pair of trousers got the same treatment, and elsewhere were neatly folded jumpers and accessories. There was not a speck of dust to be found.

The police did find one thing, though, and that was the Leeds Building Society pass book. They saw that an entry had been made on 18 February.

'Nicky, get over to the Leeds Building Society in Streatham Hill as soon as it opens this morning,' said DI Brown. 'I want to know everything that happened on the eighteenth, no matter how insignificant. Where are we on the tracksuit?'

DI Brown addressed this to no one in particular, but Jeanette answered, 'What tracksuit are you talking about?'

'It's a navy, yellow and white, with "hummel" written across the chest. Is it here?' DI Brown knew there was hardly any chance that it would be. Ferrira was too experienced to leave such incriminating evidence lying around. It must have been destroyed by now.

'I don't know the one you mean. You could always try asking his other girlfriend. Heidi's her name.' She almost spat the information out. There was no love lost between these two. This was hardly surprising as Heidi had just had her second child, and it was Ferrira's.

A couple of officers went over to question Heidi in West Norwood. Nicky went to wait outside the Leeds Building Society until it opened. The rest of the officers returned to base.

DI Brown was sure he was going to enjoy interviewing Ferrira. But this was a short-lived sensation; once Ferrira had confirmed his name, his stock reply to every question asked was 'no comment'. Why would an innocent man do that?

Right now there was little or no evidence to hold Ferrira for more than the standard forty-eight hours. I was going to have to return from Spain for a line-up. Today!

Nicky spent an age trying to get through to me on the telephone. Either all international lines were engaged or the phone at my sister's home was. Finally she reached me at four-thirty in the afternoon. 'We've got him, Merlyn. We've arrested a suspect.'

I couldn't believe my ears. This was the most fabulous news. I wanted to shout out and tell everyone, but I was in Algeciras and no one would have understood me anyway! 'How did you find him? What did you get him on? What prison is he in? What's he like?' I had so many questions zapping into my head, I needed to ask them all straight away.

I could only just hear Nicky weakly trying to halt my excesses. 'Wait a minute, Merlyn, just wait until you hear everything I've got to say. You've got to come back to England. You've got to attend a line-up.'

I didn't think I'd heard right. 'What do you mean, "attend a line-up"? You've already got him, haven't you?'

Nicky always had tremendous reserves of patience, but at that moment even hers were on low. Nevertheless the one thing she didn't do was apply any pressure. She had to get me back to London fast, but not once did she say all the things that must have been running through her mind at that point. Instead, she said, 'Look, Merlyn, I'll be honest with you. We arrested him after we got a tip-off. We've searched his flat and come up with nothing. If you pick him out of a line-up we can charge him. If you don't, he walks. Legally we can only hold him until tomorrow. Right now you're our only chance.'

Nicky had been trying to organise a flight back, but so far was unsuccessful. Lesley knew there was an evening flight from Gibraltar to London Heathrow, but would have to reach her girlfriend at the travel agency to organise it before the agency shut at 5.30 p.m.

Between Jackie at the travel agent's, Lesley and Nicky in London, a flight was booked and security for me laid on. I had not been on my own since the attack, and could not go on a

Mum and Dad, Merlyn and Reg Nuttall, just before they were married

Me, aged 10, with my stepmother, Myra Bancroft, on holiday in Jersey

My graduation photograph from Brighton Polytechnic in 1989

Effra Road in Brixton. The house with the boarded-up window is number 9 - the house I was abducted to. Note how close the bus stop is to the house *(Metropolitan Police)*

The room at the top of the house that I was attacked in

Two weeks before
the attack
*(Photograph taken
by Anthony Good)*

Two days
after the attack
*(Metropolitan
Police)*

The police artist's
impression of
Ferrira and the
tracksuit he was
wearing
*(Metropolitan
Police)*

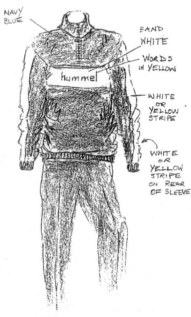

3040

3040 B

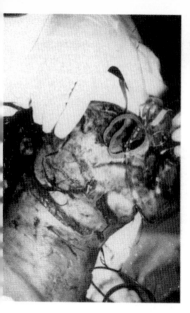

This polaroid was taken as I
entered Kings College Hospital
(Kings College Hospital)

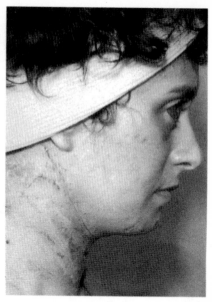

Side view of my scars one week
after the attack
(Metropolitan Police)

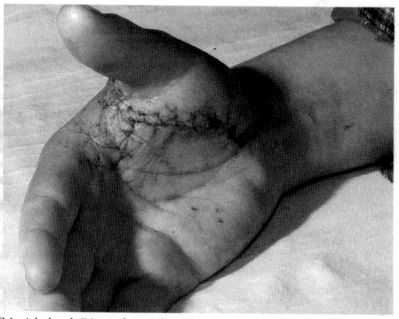

My right hand *(Metropolitan Police)*

With WPC Nicola Holding receiving her commendation for her work on my case
(Metropolitan Police)

Sisters' solidarity in hospital. Loraine, Sharon, me and Lesley

Sisters on holiday in Sotogrande, Southern Spain in 1995. Me, Lesley, Sharon and Loraine

Friends that have been a constant support - Tony, me, Chip and Heather at a friend's wedding in France and me with Andrew in February 1997

In Hollywood during my travels across America in September 1995

On holiday in Casares, Spain, 1996. Sharon and her husband, John, with their new baby, Richard

At the villa in Casares with my nieces, little Merlyn and Jennifer

plane without knowing there was someone there to 'look after me'. I arrived at the airport and was escorted on board once everyone had taken their seats. I had even been upgraded by GB Airways to Business Class. Ordinarily I would have thought how wonderful this was, but all I could think about was tomorrow. How would I react when I saw him again? What if I couldn't recognise him? I *had* to recognise him.

When I arrived at Heathrow, Sharon and Valerie were there waiting for me. We drove straight back to Camden to prepare for the big day.

John and Sharon drove me to Brixton police station early on 27 March, and we were met by John Jones and Nicky. I didn't think there was all that much to attending a line-up, but I had my eyes well and truly opened that day.

As line-up arrangements go, I understand that Brixton has one of the better facilities. The suspect and the other individuals who have been drafted in stand behind one-way glass, so they can't see out but you can see in. They each have a large number that they stand behind for identification purposes, and there is a video camera that records the whole session. The suspect's solicitor is present throughout, there is a policeman who officiates during the line-up and then there is the witness. In my case Sharon was allowed to come with me, but was not allowed to walk with me, in case it was construed that she was leading me in any way.

Before you go in, you have to wait in an anteroom. At Brixton it is because the suspect and the other people in the line-up have to use the same entrance as the witness. There was some sort of delay in holding the line-up, so we had extra time to sit and chat about what was about to happen. I listened to the police officer who was 'chaperoning' us, and took his word as gospel. 'The most important thing is to make a definite, positive ID. The faster you make it the better it looks when given in evidence.' No one said that I could ask any one of them to speak, stand up, sit down, turn around. These were all things that might have helped me check him out. Probably his appearance would have changed, and he would have been doing everything and anything to distance himself from the police artist's impression. But no one drove that point home to me. Was that because it was so obvious?

Twenty-five minutes after we arrived, a buzzer went. This was the signal to let us all know that the line-up was ready. Sharon and I stood up and were shown into a very dark, narrow corridor. A brilliant light shone through enormous panes of one-way glass, and there, standing in the brightness, were nine men. Even though I was surrounded by police, I felt petrified. The man who had tried to kill me was only yards away. What if I didn't pick him out? He could get me when I was least expecting it. I felt under so much pressure. 'I mustn't fail; I must make a quick identification – it will look better in court.' I kept these thoughts running through my mind over and over again like a mantra.

There was a policeman standing at a podium and he read out some instructions to me. He checked that I understood what I was supposed to do and I nodded. He also pointed out that the other lady present was the suspect's solicitor. He then told me I could move along the line. I walked past each man, making sure I took in all the features. But I was especially looking for his eyes, because that was all I could remember about his face from that day. There was something very familiar about number seven; he was about the right height but slightly slimmer. The eyes were wrong, though, and the hair too Afro and scruffy. He was wearing clothes that would be more suitable on someone at least twenty years older, not the street gear I would have expected him to wear. Number three was familiar too; he was wearing a tracksuit and he had a similar hairstyle to my attacker, but he was constantly looking down. I went back to number seven again, but I just wasn't sure. I needed to see number three's eyes, in fact I had to wait for him to look up, and then his eyes did seem a little bulbous.

It was a toss-up between the two of them. I went over to the policeman and said quietly and calmly, 'I think it's number three.' I had made my decision and had got it totally wrong. I'd gone for the person who looked most like my attacker did weeks ago. Ferrira was number seven.

John Jones and Nicky had been watching the proceedings on camera, and came out to commiserate with me. They must have been so disappointed, but they didn't show it. Instead they took me to a room where we could all have a cup of tea. They then told me something I didn't realise could happen in a line-up, but wished I had been made aware of beforehand: the suspect has the right to change his appearance and anybody else's in the line-up prior to the witness coming in to make an identification. The twenty-five-minute delay was due entirely to Ferrira. He had made all the other people in the line-up swap clothes. He then put on the most dowdy garments and pulled out his hair to make it look longer than six weeks' growth could achieve. Why would an innocent man do that?

One other bombshell was that the police had a total of fifteen 'volunteers' for the line-up. Ferrira was allowed to select the nine for the line-up and dismiss whichever six he wished to! Surely all of this should be admissible as evidence for the prosecution?

The police could not legitimately hold him any longer and had to release him on bail. (The bail was because he was already on probation for a drugs offence.) I felt that I had let everybody down. The police had probably pinned their hopes on a result, but it wasn't to be.

That evening Nicky and another police officer came to see me. They had two sets of photographs they wanted me to look at. First they had a set of rather blurred black-and-white photographs of a young man taken by a security camera at the Leeds Building Society. The hairstyle was similar, and so were the height and build. It was impossible to tell anything else as all the shots were in profile. I couldn't see his eyes. The second set of photographs was handed to me, and as I turned over the first one I saw those eyes again. These colour photographs were family snaps. A young man was sitting next to a white boy (Jeanette's), and was wearing a navy and yellow hummel tracksuit. His hair was in dreadlocks. The police were showing me this photograph to get a positive identification of the tracksuit, as they had not been able to find a duplicate. It was a bonus for them that I instantly recognised his eyes. This was definitely the man. It was Anthony Ferrira.

I immediately returned to Spain. All the police now had to do was to find more evidence that would enable them to re-arrest Ferrira and charge him with attempted murder. Did I say 'all'!

The police had been very lucky in getting the tip-off. Had Jeanette not come forward they would still be eliminating suspects. Now they had something positive to work with. So far all the signs pointed towards Ferrira: his past crimes were not petty misdemeanours; he was a known user; he frequented the house in Effra Road; he owned a tracksuit with 'hummel' written across the chest, and that tracksuit was missing; he had changed his hairstyle after 18 February, because the Leeds Building Society security photographs taken on the 29th showed that he had close-cropped hair, but not a flat top; finally he tried to commit suicide on the night that the *Crimewatch* programme was broadcast.

Unfortunately this body of evidence may have seemed convincing, but it was all purely circumstantial. It would never, as they say, 'hold up in court'. The police needed one piece of hard evidence, and so far all the DNA'd material had not delivered any. They would have to go back to Jeanette and Heidi and see whether they could provide any more information.

Both girls professed to love Ferrira. Both were white. Both were slim and blonde, and in their mid-twenties. Heidi occasionally worked for an escort agency, and Jeanette had a string of convictions for prostitution. There the similarities ended. Heidi was very open and giving, and a little gullible. She could not believe Ferrira could be capable of a crime like the Brixton one. She was only too happy to help the police in their enquiries, and she had no problem letting them take away her photograph albums.

Jeanette came from the Midlands. She was sure of herself and very street-smart. She had a strong and open distrust of the police yet she had informed them of her suspicions. Perversely, Jeanette was Ferrira's alibi for the morning of the attack. She was fiercely protective of and devoted to her only son.

For three days following the line-up, Ferrira did not venture out of the flat. On the fourth day, 1 April, he and Jeanette went out for the evening. They visited a club and Ferrira had quite a lot to drink. At around 1 a.m. they left and began walking home. It was not a particularly warm evening so they were walking quite quickly. Two black men were walking towards them, and when they drew level with Ferrira, one of them said, 'This is for the girl.' Then they both grabbed him under his arms and flung him through the glass window of the building he had just passed. Jeanette started screaming, and tried to pull them off him, but it was all over in seconds and the men ran off in different directions. Jeanette couldn't tell where Ferrira was hurt. He did not seem to be bleeding, but he was clearly in great pain. She ran off to call an ambulance. Once at the hospital he was examined and shards of glass were removed from his armpit and buttocks. He had sustained minor injuries to his back and arms.

'Mr Forbes, you must lie down so I can treat your wounds,' the Casualty sister said. 'Forbes' was Jeanette's surname.

'You're not going to treat my wounds, because I'm going home,' Ferrira snapped back angrily.

Now was probably not the time to use scolding, head-teacherly tones, but the Casualty sister had already had a hard night. 'Now don't be silly, unless you let me . . .'

Ferrira snapped again, but this time in his head. He jumped off the trolley, grabbed the nurse by her uniform and pushed her up against the wall of the room they were in. He snatched a pair of forceps from her top pocket and pressed them against her throat. 'I said I don't want any treatment. Can you hear me this time?' He released her, threw the forceps on the floor and walked out.

The police were called and the nurse made a statement. She wouldn't press charges, though. She unfortunately accepted that this kind of behaviour went with the territory. It's a sad reflection of life in nineties Britain that this kind of behaviour can be classed as 'acceptable'.

The police continued to put pressure on Jeanette and Heidi to give them more information. With Jeanette it was impossible to tell whether or not she knew more, but Heidi definitely did, and it was just a question of time . . .

Everyone had just about given up any hope of having forensic evidence that would point the finger at someone. And then, at the end of April, DC Mark Chapman announced to the members of the team that the scientists at the Metropolitan Police Science Laboratory now had some evidence that put Ferrira and me in the house at approximately the same time. The SOCOs had found a bloodstained white serviette on the landing of the house in Effra Road. Due to recent cleaning of the common parts, it was probable that it had not been there for long. The blood was definitely mine, but there was also a fingerprint on the serviette. They managed to lift this fingerprint off the serviette by chemically treating it. It was a time-consuming process, but it paid off in the end. The fingerprint belonged to Anthony Ferrira.

On 1 May 1992 Anthony Ferrira was arrested and charged with the attempted murder of Merlyn Nuttall.

CHAPTER 7

The Trial

Forensic science had won the day after all. It was an extremely difficult task to lift the fingerprint from the serviette, so although it was collected with all the other evidence on 18 February, it wasn't until the end of April that the scientists at the Metropolitan Police Science Laboratory were able to state conclusively that the blood was mine and the fingerprint was his.

I was buoyed up by the news. In my opinion forensic evidence was indisputably the most reliable you could get. The trial was as good as won.

I booked my ticket home.

My time in Spain had been well spent. I was more confident there. Most importantly, one of Lesley's friends, Marian Fitzpatrick, was a physiotherapist. She gave me the crucial massage and manipulation necessary to safeguard the mobility of my right hand and my neck. Every morning and evening specific exercises were given and massage applied. This treatment was designed to stop the scar tissue knitting to my bone, and eventually to rebuild and strengthen my muscles and increase their flexibility. It was painful at times, but every day I could see and feel the improvement. It was a regime that I followed twice daily for the next six months. Without it I cannot tell how limited my neck and hand movements would have been. If I had stayed in England I don't believe anything would have been done until, possibly, it was too late to do any good.

I was sad to be leaving Les and Pat and the bright, sunny Spanish days, but London was where I belonged. Besides which, before the attack I had promised to 'style' a girlfriend's wedding and make the bridesmaids' dresses. The wedding was only four weeks away, and there was so much to do. My girlfriend had waited for me through what must have been very worrying times for her, and I was not about to let her down. I was determined that whatever I had started before the attack would be completed.

Coming back to London also meant renewing my contacts with the police and Nicky. I had really missed the 'team' and the involvement. However, now that Ferrira was on remand, I knew that matters would be handled by solicitors and barristers, not the police. Their work was done for the time being.

The first stage in the legal process was the committal hearing. This was where the magistrates would make their decision, after reviewing the evidence, on whether the case was strong enough to go to a Crown Court. Hamish Brown told me I would probably need to attend the hearing and would also have to go through my statement with the magistrates. I did not relish this prospect, but, in the end, my presence was not required. (I have since found out it is not always necessary for the victim to attend committal hearings.)

The trial was scheduled to be heard at the Old Bailey on 19 October 1992. This was eight months after the attack.

To tell the truth I was very nervous about the trial; of having to dredge up all those unpleasant memories again, the memories I had spent months trying to forget. I just didn't want to give evidence. I couldn't bear the thought of having to recount to a roomful of complete strangers the most intimate details of Ferrira's assault on me. Why should they know, when only the police, Sharon and Valerie had been told exactly what had happened? Why should anybody be able to walk in from the street straight into the public gallery to listen to the fine detail? Any voyeur in town had permission to be titillated at the Crown's expense.

Then I was worried about my family. They would be in the public gallery rubbing shoulders with his family and friends, and I was naturally concerned for their safety. Ferrira came from a completely different world from ours, and to most people's, I would imagine. What if they tried to intimidate my sisters to get to me?

I was also dreading the public humiliation of being cross-examined, of people trying to 'catch me out' to discredit what I had been through, to get Ferrira off. So, when I was offered an escape route, I was sorely tempted.

Hamish Brown and Nicky had taken me to the Old Bailey, so I could see for myself what the place was like. They let me go on to the witness stand to practise speaking to the floor. The grandeur of the building and its history were not lost on me. I still didn't want to give evidence. All I wanted was a way out. And Hamish Brown was about to provide it.

'I have a bit of news that I think you'll like, and it will mean you won't have to give evidence.'

From the way Hamish Brown was speaking I felt sure he was 'testing the water' in some way.

'If we were to change the charge from Attempted Murder to

Grievous Bodily Harm With Intent, Ferrira might plead guilty. That means you won't even need to go to court.' He seemed eager that I should consider this option.

'But surely GBH, even With Intent, will carry a much lesser sentence?' I argued. 'I don't want to be forever looking over my shoulder because he got off early with good behaviour.'

I was naturally concerned because, as much as I did not want to take the stand, I didn't want to be responsible for allowing a vicious killer to be loose on the streets – for a second time.

'There is no way that can happen. GBH With Intent will carry as stiff a sentence as Attempted Murder because of the brutality of the attack. So you don't need to worry on that score,' said Hamish Brown with conviction.

I have never been an overly suspicious person, but there was something that wasn't quite right here. If the GBH charge carried an equal sentence why would Ferrira plead guilty to the lesser charge? No, there must be another reason for this change of heart, and I probably wouldn't like it.

I was right on both counts.

'Look,' said Nicky, sensing my uneasiness, 'you know I've always been straight with you? Well, you've got to listen to me and you've got to be strong. We've got a big problem with the evidence. Everything we have points to Ferrira, but it's all circumstantial. Even the serviette doesn't give us conclusive proof he was there at the same time you were. He's already admitted that he used the house at Effra Road to smoke crack, so finding his fingerprints there is no surprise. Your blood was everywhere, so why not on a serviette that had been dropped in the hallway some time ago?'

Nicky was looking at me, waiting for a reaction. My only reaction was to look confused. Why arrest him in the first place if there was insufficient evidence to put him away? And why would the magistrates at the committal hearing recommend a Crown Court?

I could see now, however, that Hamish Brown had tried to soften the blow. It was clear to me that the police and the Crown Prosecution Service didn't believe the evidence was strong enough to convict Ferrira on Attempted Murder, and that to be sure of a conviction a lesser charge was necessary.

It was mid-May 1992, a full twenty weeks before the trial date. There was more than enough time for me and my family to conduct our own investigations if need be! I was determined that Ferrira was going to go away for a very, very long time. I was feeling downright angry that anyone could consider downgrading the charge after what I'd been through.

However, I knew nothing about the legal system and, as a victim and witness, it seemed that no one was obliged to help me learn. Up to that time, I had been reliant on my DI for such information, but, as time wore on, I would increasingly question how complete that information was.

I wanted to know where we stood legally, and asked to speak to the solicitor or barrister handling the case.

'I'm sorry but that's not allowed,' said Hamish Brown. 'Any questions you may have need to go through me.'

'What do you mean, "not allowed"? If a barrister is going to ask me some extremely intimate questions, I'd like to know him [we'd established it was a 'him'] a bit better. That's not an unreasonable request, is it?'

It obviously was, and I was clearly not going to be allowed access to any legal representative. Yet it was so important that I speak to someone, especially in the light of the possible problem surrounding 'circumstantial evidence'. Dealing with Hamish Brown might be the only way to do it, but it did not fill me with confidence. There was so much I needed to know:

for example, would I have screens to shield me from Ferrira, if and when I gave evidence? He kept telling me he'd check, but never gave me a definite 'yes' or 'no'. Was this because he was being fobbed off by the solicitor or, more ominously, was he being given every indication that I would not be allowed that degree of protection? And, if I was told the truth, would I agree to take the stand?

Once, after another round of badgering Hamish Brown to set up a meeting with the barrister, I was informed that it would not be possible as the defence could construe this as 'witness coaching', and this would harm our case. How ridiculous. I was pretty certain that Ferrira would be told how to behave before the case came to trial, and I was sure the Crown Prosecution Service wouldn't utter a word against it. What a shame we wouldn't be able to introduce his behaviour before the line-up at Brixton as evidence. The legal system seemed unequal. He was allowed so much assistance, all gratis, and I couldn't even get to meet the solicitor or barrister for the prosecution.

Meanwhile I was continuing my daily telephone calls to the police station to check on forensic results, and got my usual 'nothing to report just yet' reply. In fact it seemed to me as though that was the state of play on the whole investigation. It was all slowing down.

DC Redford, or 'Jumbo' as he was more commonly known, was a huge man. He was about six feet four inches, weighed around eighteen stones, and was probably in his mid-forties. He had red hair, and a flamboyant red beard to match. He laughed a lot too, so it wasn't difficult to relax in his company. I had met him many times, and knew how much effort he'd put into the case, especially behind the scenes.

Jumbo was having a coffee with Jeanette in her flat one

afternoon when he said, 'You know the one thing that's puzzling all of us? It's his tracksuit. How can a tracksuit just disappear into thin air?'

Jumbo needed Jeanette's help as much as he needed the tracksuit. Another piece of hard evidence, and the nearer they'd be to throwing the book at Ferrira, rather than throwing the towel in. She had had the conscience to inform on Ferrira in the first place, but now that it might not be enough to hold him for as many years as they'd hoped, maybe she could help some more.

'I'm not prepared to say anything unless it's off the record,' Jeanette said after a long draw on her cigarette. She had information that could help the police, but she also had a very strong instinct for self-preservation.

'To be honest with you, Jeanette, we'll take anything you can give us, on or off the record. We need to keep this investigation alive, or, come the nineteenth of October, Ferrira could walk.' Jumbo said this without rancour; he was just telling it as it was.

Jeanette knew enough about the law to know he was right, and she wanted to help, as long as it didn't jeopardise her own personal safety or that of her son. She looked past Jumbo into the distance and started talking. 'That night he was supposed to have spent with me; he didn't. We had a row and he stormed out. It must have been about eleven o'clock. I didn't see him again until the next morning.'

'What time was that then?' Jumbo asked, leaning forward. He was trying not to look too interested, but if this information was true, Ferrira's alibi had just been smashed to smithereens.

'About nine in the morning. I noticed the time because he was acting strange. After he let himself into the flat, he came into the bedroom, but he was totally naked. I asked him where his clothes were, and he told me he'd done an aggravated burglary in East Dulwich and had got rid of them. He was breathing heavy and had scratches on his face. He had a shower, got changed and left. Tony was back in a couple of hours and he'd had his hair shaved off on top.'

'What was he wearing when he left you that night?' Jumbo asked.

'That hummel tracksuit you're after,' Jeanette replied. 'And before you ask me, no, I won't make a statement about it. I've already told you, it's off the record.'

She was as cool as a cucumber, and Jumbo knew he could only go so far before she clammed up. He had to think of a different tack; he had to find a way of getting more information.

'Where do you think he left the tracksuit then? Would he have had time to hide it in the flat?' he asked.

'He wouldn't be that stupid, would he? No, he dumped it. The binmen came that day.'

Once Jumbo had checked whether the refuse really was collected from that area on that day, and it was confirmed, the investigation got a new lease of life, and Nicky and some lucky colleagues got the opportunity to commune with nature.

Mucking is a land-fill site in rural Essex. This is where Streatham's rubbish goes to, and it's where six officers from the Incident Room were also sent in May 1992.

Their objective was to find the hummel tracksuit and my handbag, and anything else that would tie him to me. To help them achieve their objective they were given one digger, one dumper truck, one Land Rover and four refuse workers.

They were shown the area where rubbish had been deposited for the specific collection date. The officers, overalled, gloved and masked, set about excavating that part of the site. It was the most filthy job you could imagine, digging up and then sifting through metres of compacted rubbish. At the end of two weeks no evidence had been uncovered, but £15,000 had been spent trying.

It wasn't so much a case of 'back to the drawing board' as 'back to the girls'. The police knew that Ferrira was wearing a hummel tracksuit on the night before the attack, and that he no longer had it.

The police also knew that his movements on the morning of the attack were unaccounted for. So far Jeanette had been helpful but very guarded. Perhaps Heidi could fill in the gaps?

Initially Heidi, although very friendly and open, was quite reticent about offering any information on Ferrira, no matter how innocuous. Hamish Brown later discovered that this was because she had been receiving intimidating phone calls from him while he was on remand at HM Prison Belmarsh. However, she was still considered a promising witness, but the funds for the Incident Room were running out and the feeling among senior officers was very much one of 'let's go with what we've got'. The Incident Room was disbanded.

The case against Ferrira was still not watertight. I had placed all my faith in the police and I knew they weren't going to let me down.

And they didn't.

What I hadn't realised was that Nicky had begun working on the investigation in her spare time, and had asked for Mark Chapman's help. New duties had been given to all the officers involved on this case, but Nicky knew that I could not put it behind me if he was free. (One officer actually said he would resign if Ferrira wasn't convicted, because if justice couldn't serve a victim like me, who could it serve?) Call it sixth sense, call it women's intuition, Nicky knew Jeanette and Heidi had much more information on Ferrira than they were letting on.

Perhaps if they played one off against the other they might get somewhere . . .

One evening when Nicky and Mark were talking to Heidi at her flat in Norwood, she admitted that Ferrira had come to her place on Monday night, 17 February, at around eleven o'clock. He was wearing his hummel tracksuit. He stayed for a while, then took a cab home.

'When you say he left by cab, did you call one for him?' Nicky asked, hardly daring to hope she'd get the dream reply.

'No. He called the cab, but it's the one I always use,' Heidi said, oblivious to the damage this was about to do to the case for the defence.

When Nicky and Mark left the flat, they both punched the air in victory. All they had to do now was find the taxi driver and get his statement, and another piece of the jigsaw would fall into place!

Later that night they traced Sean Cremin. He opened the door, looked at them and said, without any surprise whatsoever, 'I was expecting you before now.'

On 25 September 1992, the taxi driver from Knight's Hill Radio Cars came to Brixton police station and made a formal statement. Due to the introduction of this new evidence, the trial date was postponed until 11 January 1993.

Nicky and Mark's hard work was beginning to pay off. So much of the evidence showed that Ferrira was in the right place at the right time. He was wearing a tracksuit like the one worn by my assailant only hours before I was abducted. He no longer had that tracksuit at nine o'clock that same morning. He immediately went out again and had his hairstyle changed. Sean Cremin's statement showed that en route to Effra Road he had to stop outside a café in the Loughborough Road while Ferrira got out for a few minutes. He said he had to do some 'shopping'.

Both the café and Loughborough Road were well-known places for drug dealing in the Brixton area. Then there was the serviette found in the house with my blood on it and his fingerprint – after the common parts had been swept by Slings on the Sunday night before she left. The attempted suicide after watching *Crimewatch*. And on top of all this, the inadmissible evidence, which convinced the investigating team, if no one else, of his guilt: spending twenty-five minutes rearranging the line-up at Brixton police station; refusing to say anything in police interviews except to confirm his name and his previous convictions for violence.

The biggest hole in the investigation so far was that the one person who could confirm his guilt was also his alibi for the morning of Tuesday, 18 February 1992: Jeanette.

Nicky had made up her mind that she would see her one last time and try to persuade her to give the police a little more help. She knew she was asking a lot, because as much as Jeanette loved Ferrira, he also terrified her, and she had already started receiving threats from friends of his.

When Nicky arrived at Jeanette's flat an idea was forming in her mind. She was going to try a different tack.

Jeanette made them some coffee and sat down opposite her. 'There's nothing more I can say, you know. You've got as much out of me as I'm going to give.'

Nicky smiled as she said, 'I know, and I'm not going to try. I really just want your help in solving a little mystery. You admitted some time ago that a few days after the attack was reported in the press, you went to Brixton police station and asked some very specific questions about his sexual behaviour during the attack. Can you tell me a little more about it?'

'I don't know what he did to her, but I do know what he likes to do to me when he's stoned on crack. You want to know, don't you?' Jeanette didn't wait for an answer, and just continued. 'The one thing he doesn't want is straight sex, and if he doesn't get what he wants, he's violent. He likes to bugger me and have oral sex. When he's in my mouth he always tells me to bite it.'

'Bingo!' thought Nicky. Now if she could get information from Heidi that corroborated Jeanette's story, she might just be able to convince them that they should both take the stand as witnesses for the prosecution.

Heidi's story checked out, too. (In fact, listening to both girls' accounts of their violent sexual relationship with Ferrira, Nicky felt as though she was re-reading my statement, so strong were the similarities. They both felt completely intimidated by him, and both knew that if he got off they'd suffer.)

In the end both women agreed to make statements and to appear as witnesses for the prosecution. The defence had just lost their star witness and Ferrira his alibi.

Christmas has always meant family to me, as it does to so many people. However, it had been several years since all four sisters had been together to celebrate it, but we were going to be together now. John's mother lived in a huge Georgian house in a small village in Essex. As she was going away over Christmas we took it over. Loraine and Danny came down from Manchester, Lesley and Pat flew in from Spain and Sharon, John and baby Merlyn travelled with me from London. But no matter how hard I tried, I could not enjoy the festivities. All I kept thinking was that with the New Year came the trial, the outcome of which would be pivotal to how I lived the rest of my life.

The principal source of my worry was that Jeanette and Heidi were by no means solid witnesses, and they were key to winning the case. They kept changing their minds and changing their statements. Then I had still not met either the solicitor or barrister; and no one had confirmed or denied whether I could have screens to shield me from Ferrira when giving evidence. So all in all, perhaps it was understandable that I did not feel confident about the outcome of the trial.

I was well aware that if the jury had any doubt about his guilt, they would have to release him. What would I do then?

Monday, 11 January 1993. Judge R. Lowry QC was to preside over the trial. John Nutting was the counsel for the prosecution, and Alan Suckling for the defence.

We arrived in convoy at the Old Bailey. Queuing up outside the public gallery I could see a host of familiar faces. Family and friends had turned up in droves. They were going to fill as many seats in the gallery as possible to prevent his family and friends from recognising who the immediate members of my family were and to avoid any chance of intimidation.

Sharon and Valerie were allowed to come with me while I waited to be called to give evidence – Hamish Brown told me I was going to be the first witness called. Getting through the main entrance took an age as the number of people, coupled with the security checks, slowed everything down. We'd just joined the first queue to have our documents checked when I caught a glimpse of someone a few feet ahead of me who looked frighteningly familiar. I couldn't breathe and I couldn't move. I was tugging at Nicky's sleeve. Everyone was asking me what the matter was, did I want to sit down, and all I could do was stare at this tall black guy who was the spitting image of Ferrira. When Nicky realised what was going on, she sent someone off to find out who he was. It was Ferrira's younger brother. It had been almost a year since I'd seen that face. This wasn't a picture, this wasn't a line-up, this was real, and I saw the resemblance instantly. If anyone had been in any doubt about Ferrira's whereabouts on 18 February 1992, they had only to see my reaction to his brother on 11 January 1993. But what was he doing here anyway? He wasn't a witness, he wasn't a solicitor or barrister. He should have been in the public gallery. Was he waiting for someone? Me? Jeanette? Heidi? I have since found out from the Victim Support Witness Service based at the Old Bailey that they have nicknamed this area 'the Danger Area'. All witnesses, jurors, solicitors, barristers and even defendants on bail come and go via this entrance and, while there is currently no way of separating them, there is no way of preventing Joe Public entering the lobby area either, and just waiting. I hung back in the lobby until he had disappeared, then I was shuffled through the turnstile, flanked by police and family, and taken up to the canteen. This was to be our base, as there were no other facilities at the court, until I was called to give evidence.

It was a long morning. I was given my statement to read through and then all I could do was wait. It was a strange time. I kept seeing faces that were so familiar, but couldn't work out where I'd seen them. Then they'd come over and introduce themselves, and I'd berate myself for forgetting. One person I couldn't forget, but whom I hadn't seen since that fateful day in Brixton, was Ian Crittenden. He was the firefighter who was responsible for saving my life.

Lunchtime came and went and still I had not been called. In fact I knew that if I wasn't called soon I wouldn't be called at all that day. Hamish Brown had told me that they wouldn't put me through the trauma of starting to give evidence on one day, and having to continue on the next.

Again I asked if I was able to meet the solicitor or barrister, and, slightly surprised, Hamish Brown said, 'Oh, you still want to do that?'

The afternoon wore on, and just as I was thinking that I couldn't drink any more tea or make any more small talk, I became aware of billowing black material and rustling papers briskly approaching our table. A tall, bewigged gentleman was now leaning over me, extending his hand.

'Hello, I'm John Nutting. You must be Merlyn Nuttall.' He was smiling, and I found myself smiling back. 'I'm representing the prosecution,' he continued, 'so if you have any questions or queries just ask away.' At last. But it had taken me eight months to get to the eleventh hour!

All my anxieties disappeared under his calming influence and, once he had reassured me that the defence counsel would not give me a hard time when I was on the stand, only one question remained: 'Am I going to have screens when I give evidence?'

'In fact I'm just off to discuss this matter with the Judge and Mr Suckling. So we'll have an answer shortly.' He was so charming I didn't even think about the number of times I had asked this question of the police. It was clear to me now that no one could have given me an answer until the trial was under way. Why couldn't someone have told me that?

Hamish Brown had gone with Mr Nutting and returned after about half an hour. He was smiling, so something had gone right.

'What have they said about the screens?' I asked, not even assuming there could be anything else to look pleased about.

'You've got them!' Hamish Brown replied, still beaming. 'The screens will extend from the witness entrance door to the stand itself, so you won't be able to see him. He will be able to see you on TV though.'

On hearing this, Sharon, Valerie, Nicky and I leaned forward, almost as one, thinking we had misheard.

'What TV? I don't want him to see me. I don't want to be recognised by him. That's one of the main reasons I wanted screens in the first place!' I couldn't temper the exasperation in my voice, even if this wasn't the most discreet place to have a heated discussion. 'Why is he entitled to a TV, for heaven's sake?' I demanded. I simply couldn't work out why on earth he'd need one.

'It seems the defence are concerned that your having screens will influence the jury in your favour, and therefore jeopardise their case. Allowing Ferrira to see you give evidence on a TV monitor evens it up,' Hamish Brown told me.

I actually felt sorry for Brown, because I knew there was absolutely nothing he could have done in that courtroom to influence or change any decisions.

'Anyway, I also wanted to tell you that they have called you to the witness stand,' Hamish Brown went on. 'Good luck!'

It was three-thirty in the afternoon. Panic, panic, panic. That's all I could feel. I was being walked through to the courtroom — it was the weirdest feeling. I was walking, but I wasn't. And then I was there.

From the minute I sat down, Judge Lowry did all he could to make me feel less nervous and less uncomfortable about the proceedings. From that moment my attitude changed. This was something I had to do. And I had to do it to the best of my ability. This man must never be allowed on the streets again; he must never be given the opportunity to assault anyone again and destroy their lives. I resolved to block out all the people in the courtroom staring at me; I was going to keep all my emotions at bay; and I would show that it was Ferrira who was the weak one, and that I was the stronger and more resilient.

I was sworn in and John Nutting asked me to tell the court about how my day started on the morning of Tuesday, 18 February 1992. I had had to do this many times before, but never to so many people. However, the next thirty minutes seemed to pass very quickly, as there were so many interruptions: Judge Lowry had a question here, Mr Nutting wanted me to clarify a point there. And before I knew it, Judge Lowry was saying that it was getting late and the case would be adjourned until 10 a.m. the next morning. So much for my giving evidence all in one go!

I was shattered by the day's inactivity but, strangely enough, not upset that we would have to reconvene on Tuesday. Now I knew how the land lay, physically, it was one less worry and I could concentrate on giving my evidence.

When we all got back to our Camden base it was impossible to carry on normal conversations. Everyone knew that the next day I would have to go into some fairly explicit detail about the assault. They were, naturally, feeling anxious for me. But they were also feeling a little anxious for themselves because, with the exception of Sharon, John and Valerie, no one in my family knew what I had actually been subjected to.

The next day none of us was particularly interested in eating a hearty breakfast. I think we all thought the sooner we got to the court, the sooner it would be over. It was nine o'clock, and although the Old Bailey was only a fifteen-minute drive from Camden, everyone wanted to be in the queue for the public gallery early.

It was a very quiet journey to the court. No one could even muster the small talk we'd been indulging in so much of lately. Nicky took me straight to the canteen, and we waited to be called.

During the course of my giving evidence on this day there

were, thankfully, far fewer interruptions. However, I knew when it came to specific points on the sexual assault, Mr Nutting would want to draw the jury's attention to them. And he did. The effect on my family and friends was devastating. Sharon later told me of the disbelief, the anger and the sobbing. Loraine was so distressed she had to be taken out of the public gallery by John until she had had time to calm down.

No one, in reality, was prepared for the unadorned truth.

The cross-examination was not nearly as daunting as I thought it was going to be. Mr Suckling was not trying to discredit me or my evidence, merely to prove that I was mistaken over my assailant's identity. One strategy he tried to use to achieve this was to show that I had a bad memory. (I had described my assailant as being clean-shaven, but Ferrira actually had the beginnings of a beard at the time.) Bearing in mind the accuracy with which I had described the room I was in, the tracksuit he was wearing, his hairstyle and the house, having a bad memory was probably not the best line of defence, although it may have been the only one they had.

With the cross-examination completed, I was allowed to leave the courtroom. I had been on the stand for over four hours.

Jeanette and Heidi were due to take the stand the following day, so I had my fingers crossed that they were going to stick to their guns. It would be difficult for both of them. They had already endured intimidation, and might face more during and after the trial.

Jeanette came up trumps. She was a brilliant witness for the prosecution. What made her evidence all the more credible was her obvious sincerity when she said that she still loved Ferrira.

When Heidi took the stand she corroborated the salient points that Jeanette had made earlier. What an incredible relief, but the best was yet to come. Ferrira was now going to take the stand. Up until this point we had been told that he would not be giving evidence, but with the disappearance of his star witness, there wasn't anyone else who could be called in his defence.

Apart from the two days I was required to be in court, I never went to the Old Bailey again except to hear the verdict. I wanted to hear Jeanette and Heidi give evidence. They had been so brave. But I couldn't even contemplate going into the public gallery; instead I had to rely on regular lunchtime and evening updates from family and friends. Why couldn't I have a TV monitor like Ferrira? I needed to know what was being said. I felt as though my whole future depended on it. And in a way it did.

Towards the end of the trial Sharon came home, after attending court, looking very amused. She had been there to hear Ferrira give evidence.

'What's put a smile on your face today?' I had to ask because we'd all had so little to smile about recently.

'That man does not dust!' she replied.

'Have I missed something?' I was very curious.

'Yes,' Sharon said. 'A great piece of cross-examination. John Nutting was questioning Ferrira on the sleeping pill overdose, and trying to get him to admit he had taken the pills as an act of remorse. Ferrira said it was all a mistake because he thought he was taking hay fever pills. "Hay fever pills? In March?" Nutting bellowed. Ferrira said he was allergic to dust, and he'd been dusting the flat that evening. Nutting rolled his eyes around a bit and asked, "Do you know how many hay fever pills you took? You took twenty-five of them!" The thought of this guy doing housework . . . well, it just tickled me.'

The trial lasted eight days and, despite the high points of the girls' evidence, and the various pieces of the jigsaw puzzle falling neatly into place, none of us felt confident about the outcome. We knew that the defence counsel only had to cast the smallest shadow of doubt over Ferrira's guilt and the jury would have to deliver a 'not guilty' verdict.

Sharon had gone to the barristers' summing up on the 19th, but hadn't called me to give an update during the day. When she returned home, she went straight to bed saying she had a headache. Much later she would admit to me that Nutting's summing up had been brilliant, but Suckling's was very, very good. Good enough, she thought, to cast a shadow of doubt and get Ferrira off. She couldn't tell me about it, because she didn't want to put any more pressure on me.

On 20 January at around midday I got a phone call at work (I had been back at Bhs since June 1992) from Nicky. She was at the Old Bailey. 'The jury's been sent out to decide on their verdict. They could be out for ages, but you need to be here. Can you come now?'

I was caught off-guard. No one had expected the trail to be over quite so soon. I did and I didn't want to be there. If he was found guilty I'd be the happiest person alive. If he was found innocent I'd be on the next plane to Spain.

'We'll meet you outside the Old Bailey. Call us when you're near; we're in the canteen at the moment.' Nicky hung up and I phoned for a taxi.

Nicky and Sergeant Simon Seeley were on the street to meet me. We went up to the canteen where John Jones was waiting, and we all sat down and had some tea. After about fifteen minutes John suggested we go across the road to the Magpie & Stump and have some lunch. We could be in for a very long wait.

When I walked through the doors of the pub I couldn't

believe my eyes. Everyone was there, the whole team, some of whom I hadn't seen in months. Even off-duty officers from Brixton who had nothing to do with the case felt they needed to be there on that day. They were all waiting. It hadn't been lost on me just how special this case was to all of the police officers involved. I didn't just want a guilty verdict for me, I wanted it for them too.

I was told it could be hours before the jury reached a decision. But I hadn't been in the pub more than an hour and three quarters when one of the officers received a panic call on his mobile phone. It was Hamish Brown: 'Get Merlyn over here quick. The jury's back!'

All you could see was a multicoloured streak, as about twenty people left the pub in five seconds flat. We all raced over the road, but our entrance to the courtroom was barred as court was now in session. I couldn't believe it. We were going to miss the verdict. At a suitable moment we were allowed to go in. Nicky, Sharon, Valerie, John Jones, Simon Seeley and I managed to sit down in a row together. Hamish Brown was on the stand, but I couldn't make out what he was saying.

'What's he doing there?' I whispered to Nicky. 'What's going on? They haven't given their verdict already, have they? Are we too late?' Hamish Brown was reading out Ferrira's past offences to the jury.

Nicky squeezed my hand and whispered back, 'We've got him.'

It had only taken the jury two hours to reach a unanimous decision. Ferrira was found guilty on all charges.

Sentencing followed after a few minutes' deliberation. Judge Lowry gave Ferrira twenty years for the attempted murder, eight years for the indecent assault and five years for the kidnapping. These sentences were to run concurrently, which meant he was given twenty years to serve in one of Her Majesty's prisons.

I summoned up the courage to look at Ferrira – the only time I dared to look at him (the line-up aside) since I first saw him in Effra Road in 1992. He looked so puny sitting there, and it upset me that such a pathetic creature could have wreaked such havoc in my life and in so many others' lives.

It didn't matter that we were in the courtroom. Everyone was so happy, relieved and emotional. I raced round to the jury members and thanked each of them. I think they were almost as relieved as I was. Everyone was hugging or kissing or crying or a combination of all three. I couldn't cry but I was elated that everyone else's tears were tears of joy. Sharon leapt up and hugged John Nutting.

'Merlyn, do you feel up to making a statement to the press?' John Jones was at my side. 'I know you've got things to say, and this is your platform to say them. Tomorrow will be someone else's.'

I knew I had things to say, too, but right now the one that came to mind was 'make mine a double'! I felt so obliged to the police, though, and I felt such absolute trust for John Jones, that I would have done anything to help them. It's true I did have things to say, but I couldn't think of one of them at that precise moment.

'Of course I will.' I'd never had to deal with the press before, but over the next few days I was going to have a crash course.

None of the interviews was for money. The initial interviews were conducted outside the Old Bailey, as is the norm, while the rest of my party reconvened in the Magpie & Stump. John Nutting came in for a drink as well. His summing up then over a glass of wine still rings in my ears: 'It was important to win this one.'

CHAPTER 8

Compensation

In 1995 WPC Leslie Harrison was stabbed through the heart with a screwdriver when she attempted to arrest a drug addict. She subsequently received £40,000 from the Criminal Injuries Compensation Board (CICB) one year later, but not before she had to undergo the humiliation of having to remove her blouse in front of three elderly male barristers to show them the extent of her injuries. She had photographic evidence, but they apparently needed to see the real thing.

In February 1995, three years after Ferrira's attack on me, my hearing with the CICB was held. To my amazement and disgust, I was asked by three elderly male barristers judging my case to approach their table, lift up my hair and show them the injuries to my face and neck. My barrister tried to intervene: 'I have all the photographs here if you'd care to look at them.'

But they didn't care to look at them, they wanted to see me. They all stood up and crowded around me to get a closer look . . .

A few days after I had left hospital back in February 1992,

Chief Superintendent John Jones visited my sister's home in Camden and asked me if I had heard about the Criminal Injuries Compensation Scheme. As I hadn't, he asked an officer to make sure I got all the necessary forms, and advised me that I should seek the help of a barrister immediately. It sounded expensive and, as I didn't know what was going to happen with my job and my income, I filed it away at the back of my mind. I later wished I hadn't.

The CICB came into existence in 1964 to provide financial support for victims of crimes of violence. The money comes from the Government (via the taxpayer). Over the years the scheme has been revised and modified, though not always for the better. One thing that hasn't changed is the extreme difficulty in obtaining guidelines to help a 'victim' understand exactly what is required in terms of evidence; how it should be presented; how long the process should take from application to award and/or hearing; and who can help you. I almost got the feeling that that is exactly how the CICB like it. Why else would they continue to cloak their activities in such secrecy? (In fact the apparent lack of information about how to apply was based on the original idea that the Scheme was *supposed* to be simple and straightforward, so that applicants would not need representation. Over time, as the Scheme became more and more complex, victims who had access to legal advice always achieved greater awards.)

Many months later when I began to compile the evidence necessary for the CICB, I realised I was floundering, and badly. I was trying to get my own life back in order, and found myself unable to cope with the minutiae of the documentation required. I sought the help of a firm of solicitors to whom I had been introduced by a friend. They had recently won the highest ever compensation award for one of their clients, and they agreed to work for me on the understanding that I would pay their fees once compensation had been awarded.

One of the first things they advised me to do was to prepare a detailed report of all my expenditure connected with my 'recovery'. They provided me with an outline of how a solicitor would present the information. It was mind-blowing. I could not believe what I was eligible to claim for. For example, the mileage to and from my various hospital, physiotherapy and counselling visits (adjusting the costs according to the engine size of the car I was driving); the cost of every treatment or medication I had paid for; storage costs for my belongings from my flat in South London; my loss of earnings, including my loss of promotion prospects. This information had to be backdated to the period just after the attack and, as the application was filed with the CICB six months later, I had to rely on my memory, my friends' memories, my diary and my receipts.

My solicitors then organised the preparation of a Nursing Report. This was a crucial document covering my past, present and future care and equipment needs. It accounted for every penny I had spent and, more importantly, would continue to spend, on my care and convalescence. It covered everything from the additional cost of security at Sharon's house – for example, the installation of exterior sensor lights – to the cost of a 'night sleeper', which was the role my sisters played for many, many months, both here and in Spain. The report was compiled by nursing consultant Tessa Gough RGN. (Thankfully she too agreed to take her payment once the CICB had made their award.) It was extremely thorough and I believe it reinforced not just the seriousness of my claim, but my attitude towards it. I wouldn't have thought to do this, let alone known how to approach it. I was glad I had professional guidance, not to mention a sympathetic understanding of my financial situation!

To keep costs down, we agreed that I would take on some tasks, and the firm would keep a watching brief. Therefore, I would be dealing directly with the CICB claims officer handling my case. I was now about to experience one of the worst examples of bureaucratic ineptitude (and I've experienced a lot over the past four years) I have ever encountered. For every step I took forward, after one phone call to this officer, I went back two. I was desperate for money, mainly because the continuing surgery to my neck was so expensive, and I hoped that I could finalise the claim with the CICB. My claims officer was aware of this and said he would contact my surgeon as he 'needed a little more information'. When I was making a follow-up call to his office, he told me he had not made contact with my surgeon yet as, 'I know how busy these people are, so I thought I'd leave it another few weeks.' A few weeks! How was I going to pay my bills *this* week? Over the many months that we spoke and wrote to each other, not once did I get the impression he had got to grips with my case. It was continually frustrating, but I had to persist if I was to have the right quality and quantity of information for the Board.

As this thankless but necessary task progressed slowly, I began to realise that while all the information had to be clearly laid out and organised for the hearing, this, on its own, would not be enough. I knew from watching the Crown's barrister, John Nutting, in action at Ferrira's trial, that I would need someone of that calibre to represent me. I also knew from my own investigations that a barrister would cost upwards of £2,000 a day.

However, Lady Luck struck again: I met Carmel Perry and Christopher Kay, a producer/director team, when I was interviewed on one of their programmes and through them I came to be introduced to Helena Kennedy QC. I was surprised when she told me that she knew about me and had been following my case with some interest. After all, her reputation as a barrister went before her, as did her stance on women's rights. I was completely bowled over when she offered to represent me at the CICB for free!

The date for the hearing loomed. I wasn't just nervous, I was feeling physically sick. I didn't know what to expect or what was expected of me. Due to the lack of information emanating from the CICB about the CICB, and my inability to find, and therefore talk to, anyone who had been in the same or a similar situation, I might have been forgiven for looking on the CICB as some sort of secret society. There were so many unanswered questions: was this going to be another trial, except that this time I was the accused? What if they made me a paltry award (and enough people had hinted that this was going to be the case); how would I cover my growing overdraft? How would I honour my other debts to all the people who had been helping me in good faith?

The hearing was scheduled for Monday, 26 February at 2.30 p.m. At 3.30 p.m. on the preceding Friday, I had met Helena at her Chambers for a briefing meeting. While a lot of the meeting was about fine detail, the aspect of the hearing that worried me most was a comment Helena made about how I looked. For people who didn't know me I was, to all intents and purposes, fully recovered: I was coherent, confident, gregarious even; I was not a dishevelled, teary-eyed shadow of my former self. And I was determined that Ferrira was not going to make me a victim for the rest of my life.

There was absolutely no way I was going to walk into the CICB the following Monday playing the part of the stereotypical victim: frail, frightened or in any way distraught. Nervous I could do; no problem!

I had agreed to give an exclusive interview to Duncan Campbell, chief crime reporter at the *Guardian*, directly after the hearing. My reason for doing this was to highlight what I believe to be the absurdity of the legislation the Home Secretary had tried to introduce in April 1994 to compensate the victims of violent crime. The proposed scheme of compensation would be tariff-based; in other words a set amount would be payable for a specific injury. For example: £7,500 for rape; £7,500 for a broken kneecap (how can the two be compared?) and £1,250 for a dislocated finger. No account would be taken of a victim's pain and suffering, or loss of earnings. There would be no right of appeal against the level of an award. (The House of Lords deemed that the way in which this scheme was introduced was unlawful, and the Home Secretary had to withdraw it. In April 1996 a modified scheme was introduced. It is still tariff-based, but does take loss of earnings into account – after a twenty-eight-week period has elapsed.)

The date of my application to the CICB meant that I came under the 'old' scheme, whereby my application would be individually assessed by a member of the Criminal Injuries Compensation Board (made up of experienced lawyers), and based loosely on the amounts awarded for injuries by the civil courts. So, as much as I was berating a scheme which seemed sluggish, inordinately bureaucratic and out of touch, it was the better one from my point of view.

The taxi pulled up outside Morley House, in the Holborn Viaduct. Sharon and I made our way up to the second floor to await Helena Kennedy, her pupil and my solicitor. Sharon thought the reception area was reminiscent of her student common room in the seventies: carpet tiles, low-level seating, fluorescent lights; lots of fluorescent lights! The only difference was the quiet. It was church-like, and the atmosphere made us whisper rather than chat at a more audible level. However, I could not think of anything to say at that point, as my nerves had got the better of me.

Into this harshly lit arena strode an attractive, grey-haired, forty-something man, dressed in cords, rollneck jumper and leather coat. 'This must be Duncan Campbell,' I thought. As a photographer was standing on one side of him and Helena Kennedy on the other, it was a fairly safe assumption. He introduced himself and asked if his photographer could take some pictures. I was unprepared for this, but anything that could take my mind off what was going to happen next was a welcome diversion. The diversion quickly turned into farce. A very tall, very thin, very suited gentleman started to walk towards us. He was clearly angry, but was trying hard to contain himself.

'Excuse me, have you been given permission to take photographs here?' he asked the photographer. The gentleman looked calm enough, but his breathing was increasingly heavy. Before the photographer could respond, Duncan was at his side.

'We're terribly sorry, we didn't know we weren't allowed to take photographs. We're from the *Guardian*.' Duncan extended his hand to the outraged gentleman, but the latter just ignored it and carried on spluttering about having them 'removed from the building', and how 'they couldn't carry on like this here'. If Duncan apologised once, he apologised one hundred times, but it only seemed to make matters worse.

This was awful for me. I hadn't expected a scene like this to precede the proceedings. I wanted it to stop. Duncan and the photographer then offered to leave, and the gentleman walked away, shaking his head in disbelief at the audacity of the press.

Another point worth mentioning here, as it is concerned with 'publicity', is that one week before the hearing, and while

I was still at my sister Lesley's house in Spain, the programme *Crime Monthly* ran an update on my attack. There was an extensive interview with Detective Inspector Hamish Brown, who explained how all the forensic and other evidence was compiled to build a case against Ferrira. The programme showed excerpts from the reconstruction too, with Valerie playing me. During the course of the next two hours someone on the Board would bring this up, assuming that the woman featured was actually me. However, I had nothing to do with the programme except that I had given my consent for its broadcast.

The next moment Helena was at my side, telling me, 'We're on.'

We were led into another harshly lit room (obviously a boardroom), where four sets of tables had been arranged all facing into the centre of the room. Sharon and I were seated on one side with our legal representatives to our right. The tables to our left we assumed were for the barristers, and opposite us was another set of tables.

We were all talking in hushed tones, but I was desperately trying to calm the butterflies in my stomach, which had just taken to doing Morris dancing in hobnailed boots. The door opened, and in walked three gentlemen. They introduced themselves to us. They would be hearing the case, and making a decision on the amount of the award. Following on behind them was a young lady who was there to take minutes. Following her was the gentleman we had already met in reception. He was the Board's advocate, and was intimately involved in the fine detail of the case. He would be using his knowledge to advise the lawyers. 'Oh no,' I groaned inside, 'why me?'

The first hour was taken up with verification of the evidence submitted, where I was asked questions such as: 'Why do you need a mobile phone?'

'Why do you have to have a car?'

'Why was your surgery carried out privately and not on the NHS?'

I had supplied all this information to the Board weeks earlier, so I couldn't understand why they were asking me all over again.

Then they brought up the subject of publicity . . .

'Haven't you just appeared in a television programme?' the advocate mused. He then mumbled something to the panel about the earlier incident in the reception area, but I didn't catch what he said.

I explained my involvement with the programme, and that the woman in the programme wasn't me. Nevertheless I felt uneasy. It was left unsaid, but there was a very definite assumption that I was being paid for 'publicity'. The truth is that I never got paid. I appeared in public whenever I believed it was the right thing to do, and because I didn't want what I had been through to be wasted. Someone, somewhere would benefit from my experience, I hoped. However, I believed the mere mention of 'publicity' had already reduced my award.

Then came the moment I had never expected to come. They asked to see my injuries! And this request was made knowing what I had been through, knowing how sensitive I felt about my scars – I'd already spent a small fortune on plastic surgery trying to reduce them. Given that not one of them had any medical qualifications, what right did they have to do this? Helena's attempts to introduce very recent photographs of my injuries fell on deaf ears. I felt demeaned and offended by this request. However, I also felt that I could not refuse at this stage. But now I wonder why there wasn't a female representative on the panel. Why was I again made to feel a victim at the hands of a man?

The Board said they wanted to have a private 'chat', so they disappeared for a short while. They returned to inform us that they had made a decision on the award for 'General Damages', which was a sum of £30,000. A decision on 'Loss Of Earnings' would be made at the end of the week because one of the panel had to leave for a function later that afternoon. After three weeks of waiting, a few more days wouldn't harm me, I thought. But how much better I would have felt if they had had the sensitivity to say originally that they would need more time to make that decision. I would be returning to Gibraltar within two days, so they would have to contact me there. I felt so disappointed. Another system that had been established to help me had let me down just like many others.

Before the member of the board left for his appointment, he stood up, and smilingly congratulated me on having got on so well. 'You are clearly a high flyer. You'll be back working in London within the year!' For a person who must have come into contact with some of the most heartbreaking cases, this one remark demonstrated an almost total lack of understanding of the psychological and physical trauma I had been experiencing for the past three years.

Two days later, after I had already left for Gibraltar, I was notified by my solicitors that the award for 'Loss of Earnings' was £46,101. I had received a total of £76,101 damages, the highest award ever given by the CICB to a rape victim.

Initially I could not feel anything but elation. Far from being a pittance, this amount would clear all my debts and leave a little over for me to invest. Once the euphoria had worn off though, I began to realise that this kind of award would take care of the present, but what about my career in fashion which had been so abruptly ended? What about the cost of my continuing scar reduction surgery? What about the rest of my life?

Of the £76,000, deductions totalling £20,650 were made to

repay my surgical/medical, psychiatric, legal and banking debts. I have invested the rest, save for a little I keep in my current account. I have no job and no source of income. I eat into my investment periodically for large expenses – car servicing, et cetera – so, in real terms, it is dwindling.

However, I am one of the lucky ones. I used my contacts and made new ones. I was given first-class help, guidance and advice for a fraction of the market cost. I was allowed to spend money that I didn't have, thanks to my family and my bank manager, to get me back into shape physically and mentally. My confidence is growing daily.

But what would have happened without those support systems? Would I really have received record damages if I hadn't employed a firm of solicitors; if I wasn't able to engage the services of a top-flight QC? And that was before the introduction of the new tariff-based legislation.

In 1996 Terry Brownbill sued the police, claiming he had been assaulted, falsely imprisoned and prosecuted maliciously. The arrest happened after he refused to give his name or address or answer questions about a tax disc. He was awarded damages of £150,000.

CHAPTER 9

Support

'. . . now things are back to normal, you can get on with the rest of your life . . .' If I had a pound for every person who said that to me after the trial, I'd be a very rich woman indeed.

'The rest of your life' is a long-term concept. I no longer think that way. I make the best of each and every day, because that is the only way I can now live. Normality is never going to be restored. However, I have learned to accept that fact, though many of my family, friends and acquaintances find the idea more difficult to handle.

Experiencing personal tragedy on the scale that I did is, mercifully, very rare. To this day I don't know whether I have dealt with it well or not – I don't have too many points of comparison! I do believe that being 'strong' or 'weak' is *not* the only criterion for survival or failure. A confident, outgoing person, with very high self-esteem, can as easily be completely crushed by something like this as an introvert, with a very low sense of self, can gain an inner strength that was not previously there.

I know from talking to others who have suffered violent physical or mental abuse that how they have fared has been determined by another important factor: the quality of their support systems. What are these 'support systems'? They are anything or anyone that can help a victim overcome or remove obstacles that will prevent their 'healing'.

Unfortunately it is quite normal for close friends and family to assume that it is the victim's emotional welfare that is paramount. Once that has been sorted out, you'll be 'OK'. They'll look for tell-tale signs of a breakdown; they'll treat you with kid gloves; they'll talk to other people about you, but not to you about you; they'll be walking on eggshells around you, and they will expect you to feel as they might in the same situation.

Looking after the practical issues is, in fact, every bit as important, because the practicalities of life will always have an impact on the emotional side. For example, you may need to take time off work to recuperate, to help police with their enquiries, or just to go away. But how can you do any of this if your job isn't going to be kept open for you? Do you need that kind of stress on top of everything else?

I have learned a lot over the last five years. Some good things, some bad things. I struggled with public services that were inconsistent at best and totally useless at worst. There is an ideal in terms of the level of support a victim should get. That differs depending on the person. In my opinion everyone should get the very best there is. Getting the best should not be dependent on how vocal you or your family are, or how well-connected you are, or how bright or wealthy you are. It should be your fundamental right.

There have been recent changes such as the introduction of the Victim's Charter in 1996, which aims to help the victims of violent crime, most specifically in the areas of information, communication and, to a degree, protection. But why should the commendable intentions of the Charter be upheld when there is no accountability attached to them? I am not cynical about the Charter, just realistic. Still, it's early days.

Writing this book has, of course, been cathartic for me, but that had never been the intention. I wanted to explode myths, draw attention to hypocrisy, and cut through bureaucracy. I would not have embarked upon it unless I felt it could benefit survivors like me, as well as their families and friends.

However, there are others I want to reach too, and they are the people responsible for running the support systems: the National Health Service, the police force, the judiciary, Victim Support, The Rape Crisis Centre, employers, social services and others.

If this book can change one opinion, or influence one decision, then my suffering will not have been in vain.

The National Health Service

In an emergency I don't believe anyone could outperform the NHS. There is no doubt that I was in a life or death situation; time was not on my side and the Casualty staff brought me back from the brink.

I was rushed into King's College Hospital's Casualty at around 9 a.m., transferred to a trolley and treated immediately. Nevertheless, I was only wearing a thin heat-retaining sheet — the sort that looks like tin foil — and bandages on my feet to keep them warm, and I remained on that trolley and under that sheet for the next six and a half hours, until a bed was found for me. I had gaping neck wounds; I couldn't swallow my own saliva; I was in so much pain I couldn't sleep and I was acutely aware of everything going on around me.

After care

Almost two weeks after the attack I had to go back to King's College Hospital, to their outpatients department, and have the stitches removed from my hand.

First I had to go back to south London, which didn't make me feel very comfortable. Then I had to brave the crowded out-patients waiting room. Having to wait my turn with people I didn't know made me feel worse still, even though I had John and Chip with me. There should have been an appointments system which allowed 'sensitive' patients to be seen straight away, or at least be able to wait privately.

The second time I had to return to the hospital was weeks later. I had been referred by Sharon's doctor to see the Plastic Surgery Consultant there. I was concerned on a number of counts: I could barely move my right hand since the operation, the scars around my neck were unsightly and were getting bigger, there was a numbness down one side of my face, and my face was drooping on that side too. I thought he was extremely unsympathetic; his opening comment was that he remembered me because on the day I was admitted he had had to change his schedule round. (I surmised that I had been a huge irritation to him.) He examined my hand and told me more surgery would be necessary to give me a greater degree of mobility but, as far as my neck was concerned, he would prescribe a course of steroid injections. These would be injected into the keloid that had developed under my chin. (A keloid is an over-production of collagen that builds up to form too much skin.) So much skin had formed on my neck that the scar sagged under its own weight, and looked very much like a turkey's wattle. The steroids would make the scar flatter, but wider. I remonstrated that making the scar flatter and wider was not the same as making it disappear, and I didn't want this constant reminder of the attack literally hanging around my neck. He told me that there was nothing else they could do about it or the other scars on my neck, and plastic surgery was out of the question. Physiotherapy again wasn't mentioned.

I then learned that I was not being seen by Mr Mercer, the Plastic Surgery Consultant at all, but by the Registrar, Mr Huinzah!

I wrote to Mr Mercer to question the treatment prescribed. All I got in response was a letter endorsing the Registrar's recommendations.

Before leaving for Spain I visited Sharon's GP. Unfortunately it seemed to me that he had never had to deal with a situation of this sort before, and was possibly in shock himself. Consequently he could not offer any advice or give me any useful information. He could have discussed counselling, further surgery, plastic surgery, physiotherapy. He did none of these things.

When I revisited Sharon's surgery on my return from Spain, I saw a different doctor. He was completely different from the one I had seen previously – like a breath of fresh air. He was able to examine my neck and hand and discuss my options. And he was the one who recommended that I be referred to a Consultant Plastic Surgeon at King's (he suggested that hospital because they had all the relevant medical records).

I told him I was worried about contracting AIDS. Although he said that I was more likely to contract hepatitis due to the cuts I had sustained in such a filthy room, he felt I should still be checked out on both counts. He then gave me an incredible piece of advice: go privately for an HIV test. He reasoned that if I ever applied for insurance or possibly a mortgage or anything where my medical records could be requested, they would show that I had had an HIV test. As no reasons for the test are ever given, I would automatically be considered a high risk candidate.

I had the test done privately and I'm clear.

After my disastrous visit to the 'Consultant', I returned to the same GP, who suggested I get a second opinion from another Plastic Surgeon, again privately, before getting a referral to a second NHS Consultant. That way I would know exactly what surgery could achieve. He was certain that I was eligible for plastic surgery. By chance I had already heard of a plastic surgeon, through a friend of Sharon's, who was keen to help. I was given a free consultation with Miss Christina Tattari at her Harley Street clinic. She was jolly, she was unafraid of what had happened to me and she gave me hope. Yes, through a series of operations she could make the scars on my neck much smaller, less noticeable. For the first time in weeks it was explained to me that I shouldn't worry about the numbness to the side of my face: this was perfectly normal when muscles had been cut as mine had; feeling would eventually return as the muscles recovered. The drooping of my face wasn't 'drooping' at all, but merely taut skin caused by the surgeons having to pull the skin on my face down to neaten and sew together the wounds on my neck. My skin would become more elastic over time and my face would not look lopsided.

After meeting Christina, I didn't want to go to another NHS hospital for a consultation and risk being disappointed again; I didn't want to be given treatment grudgingly; I wanted Christina's skill, no matter what it cost.

It was hugely important to look normal again. I had no

money, so I borrowed it from Sharon and John to pay for the operations (until I was able to get some interim payments from the CICB), and embarked on a series of operations that were to span three years.

Looking 'normal' on the outside was easy to judge; being 'normal' on the inside was altogether more difficult to gauge. Therefore when counselling was offered, I took it, albeit reluctantly. Every six weeks I saw Professor Cawley, a psychiatrist, and he helped me more than I can say. When everyone was judging me, he remained impartial. When everyone was expecting me to crack, he kept telling me how well I was doing.

After the trial Professor Cawley recommended a trained counsellor to me and I began to see her on a weekly basis. As time wore on, I found that an hour a week working through my feelings with someone totally independent was time well spent. It helped me to put relationships and events into perspective, and that would have been impossible to achieve on my own.

Had I realised how counselling worked, I might not have been so reluctant in the first place. Perhaps that's because my perception was that counselling was used to cure things that had already gone wrong, rather than to prevent them from happening in the first place.

I didn't ask for counselling because I didn't think about counselling; it was set up for me by my employers. What if it hadn't? How would I have known if I needed it?

The Police

The police gave the investigation 110 per cent. I felt that they were sensitive to me and kept very little from me. They therefore got the best from me, and vice versa.

The only blot on their copybook was the forensic medical examination. I now find it totally unacceptable that a man, just because he was next on the rota, should have been called upon to take intimate samples from me directly after the attack. I feel strongly that there should be a provision for female rape victims and victims of sexual assault to be examined automatically by a female doctor.

How I wish I could have had some kind of aide-memoire or prompt in my hand when I was attending the line-up, so I could have reminded myself what I was and wasn't allowed to do during it. The task was a very daunting one for me. I think it is important that this aide-memoire contains the obvious and less obvious information. For example: 'Remember the suspect is likely to have drastically changed his appearance since you last saw him', and 'You can ask anyone in the line-up to speak'. I would dearly have liked to ask them all to say: 'My girlfriend's pregnant'.

The Press

Directly after the trial, and the following day, I felt under pressure to give certain press interviews, so I gave them. The pressure came from the police who, understandably, wanted media coverage of the successful conclusion to a high-profile case. They also felt that to leave it for longer than a day or so would make it old news, of no interest to anyone.

I should have stood my ground and waited, because I believe I would then have given a more considered and therefore helpful response. Ironically it would also have saved me from having to take legal proceedings against a journalist, because he 'sold his notes to a mate', after sitting in on an exclusive interview at the Police Press Officer's request. His version of the interview appeared in a TV listings magazine. It was written in the first person, so it looked as though I'd done it myself, and had received a cash payment for it. Colour pictures of me in Casualty had been used that were particularly disturbing. None of my friends had seen me like that, and some found it extremely distressing. One of my girlfriends had nightmares about it for months afterwards. The first thing I knew about it was when a friend showed the article to me at work.

It appeared just a few weeks after the trial, on the first year's anniversary of the attack.

To this day I feel uncertain about how to deal with the press. They can be pioneering; they can be campaigning; they can be caring but, like any business, they buy and sell products. You have to remember that you are not just any product; you are a highly prized brand and if the press want your story, and you're prepared to give it, it should only be on your terms. If you want copy approval, make it a condition of the agreement and get it in writing. The same goes for headline and photographic approvals.

The Judiciary

Throughout the entire investigation the only times I felt people weren't being honest or open with me were when I asked about the trial. I was continually frustrated by the lack of response I was getting. Even though the Crown was prosecuting and I was merely a witness, I was a fairly important one. Yet I was made to feel like a pawn, and certainly not worthy enough to meet the solicitor or barrister.

A face-to-face meeting with a legal representative who could tell me exactly what I was allowed to know and by when, who I was allowed to meet beforehand, and if not why not, would have been very useful and comforting to me. This kind of guidance should then be backed up by an easy-to-read (in other words devoid of any legalese) leaflet that could be kept and referred to.

The thought of attending the trial, giving evidence, and facing my attacker again, made me feel panicky in the extreme. The feeling was heightened by the presence of my attacker's brother only a few feet from me as I was queuing to enter the court on the very first day of the trial. I should have been protected from a situation like that. Every victim should be protected from a situation like that.

The Support Agencies

When the police brought Sharon to the hospital on the day of the attack, one of the doctors and one of the police officers handed her scraps of paper with a couple of handwritten telephone numbers on. One was a Rape Crisis number and the other was for Victim Support. She hadn't seen me yet, so she wasn't going to do anything until after she had. She didn't know what they could do, or how they could help, but she felt she ought to ring – just to be on the safe side. She rang them later that day. One number rang and rang, and the other had an answerphone. She left a message, but no one ever rang back. So much for support.

(I now know that many of these services rely on volunteers and have insufficient funding to serve the public as fully as they need to.)

There was nothing at the hospital that could prepare me, or my family and friends, for what lay ahead in the first few frightening days. We needed to know what was normal in such an abnormal situation. We needed to know for our own peace of mind. It would have given us something to hold on to.

The only advice and information we had received, excluding that on the police investigation and my medical condition, was contained on those two scraps of paper.

Employers

I was so lucky. My employers were Bhs, and they were the perfect employers to have in the situation I was in. First they let me know that my job was safe. Then they put up an anonymous £5,000 reward for any information that would lead to the arrest of my assailant. When I was out of hospital they organised and paid for private sessions with a psychiatric assessor, to evaluate my needs. I continued to receive my salary while I was off work for two and a half months. When I returned to work I was given a company car and a director's car-parking space right outside the building. This gave me a feeling of independence, and a lot of security. They allowed me to work flexible hours so I could fit in my numerous medical visits and my meetings with the police.

I cannot think that any other employer would have been so understanding and so generous. Is it because they employ so many women that they're more experienced at it than others? I don't have an answer but I know I was very, very lucky.

Do employers have a 'plan of action' to deal with employees who have been victims of sexual assault? Is it updated regularly? Do they have the right contacts? Do they keep abreast of the relevant legislation? Shame on those who don't. Care and expertise in this area could make all the difference to an employee's ability to recover and face the world again.

Safe and Sound

When I travel now I need to be in control, so I feel much safer driving my car, rather than travelling by train or Tube – yet car parks are frightening places. I can't use them if I'm on my own. So while I now find travelling easy, arriving and leaving can be tricky.

I tried to get a disabled sticker so I could park in well-lit areas, near people and amenities, but was turned down on the basis that I wasn't suffering from a permanent disability. I took to travelling by Ladycabs, a taxi company with only female drivers, but it was too expensive to keep using. I then learned from a friend about taxi discount cards so, while I was living in London, I would be able to travel relatively cheaply by black cab. Only a limited number are issued, and I was told that when applying for one that I would have to play on my physical disabilities and not my mental ones. It seems that discount cards are only issued on the basis of physical disability. So I talked up my physical disabilities and got the card. I would rather have got it by being straight with the local authority.

Before the attack, I had never had a mobile phone. Now I need one to keep in touch, but perhaps not in the way you might think. In the early days I needed it almost as a form of personal protection. I was frightened to travel on my own, but I knew I had to do it. So, if I was travelling in a taxi I would call someone to let them know where I was, but really it was to let the taxi driver know I'd done so. Because I regarded travelling on my own with such terror I always used the mobile phone to talk through my movements, with a friend or one of my sisters, as I was getting out of the car, opening the gate, putting my key in the lock, et cetera. I would even talk to an answerphone if no one was there – it made me feel a little more confident, and gave me a sense that I wasn't doing this completely on my own. Also it meant there was 'evidence' of where I was at a particular time, should something happen to me.

Now my mobile phone is my best friend. I will not go anywhere without it but, like the car, it costs money to buy and run.

I don't believe there is very much I could have done to prevent Ferrira attacking me. However, something definitely should have been done by the 'authorities' to keep a persistent offender, and one who had committed manslaughter at that, off the streets.

Time after time we hear of dreadful cases where someone loses their life because someone else, who should not be allowed to live amongst ordinary human beings, has been released into an unsuspecting society. Or worse still, is known to be a danger, is known to be a time bomb, but the laws that protect decent folk protect him or her too.

My sister has three young children, and she frets, like every mother must fret, about the ugly world she's brought her children into. All she wants to do is to allow them to grow up independent, loving, happy and aware. But how do you do that from a fortified turret?

Who is going to give Sharon and every mother the hope that the future will get better?

Family and Friends

Last but not least, and arguably the most important support of them all, was the network of family and friends. They were around before the attack, and hopefully will be there long after the police, the doctors, the judiciary and the press have disappeared.

For me the unconditional love I got from everyone was the

best medicine of all. Without it I do not believe I would have made the fast recovery I did. I marvelled at how this disaster in my life drew them all together and consolidated them into a protective force around me.

With the passage of time that need for total protection naturally withers, but I still need their love. It was their love that helped to sustain me through the difficult times, and keeps me looking forward to all my tomorrows.

CHAPTER 10

Postscript

After the attack I made up my mind that I would proceed with all the plans I had made before it, and take advantage of suitable opportunities that might present themselves. I made a mental list, and put this book at the top of it.

First I had to deal with the unexpected. John and Sharon decided to leave London for the country. The attack was the main reason for the drastic change of scene and, as Sharon was pregnant with her second child, they felt ready to exchange the fast pace of the city, its population, its lack of community, for a more rural existence.

I had also become increasingly frustrated by my job as a buyer at Bhs. I could not give 100 per cent. It was impossible to travel on my own to see suppliers in England, let alone to go on all the international buying trips, which are so crucial to the job. Bhs were brilliant and said I could transfer back to my old role within the design department. Everything was set up when I found out that the whole design group was about to be made redundant. I could have remained in buying; instead I took a sharp intake of breath and voluntary redundancy. In August 1993 I moved with Sharon and John to John's family home on the East Coast of England.

It was hard to leave all my friends in London, and the lifestyle I so enjoyed there, but the only place I felt truly comfortable was wherever Sharon and her family were. However, family life and all that it entails – school runs, mealtimes, stories, bath-times, bedtimes – when it's not your life, can become a little onerous.

I had been on my own for several years previously and had enjoyed the automony. Ultimately I needed to find my way back to that state of mental and physical independence, but I recognised that it wouldn't be easy.

I flew to Spain to spend some time with Lesley and Pat and try to prioritise my plans. By chance I was offered a job setting up and launching a restaurant and brasserie in a new marina in Gibraltar. I knew my student training would come in handy one day! I grabbed it with both hands. I would be working on an exciting venture, in a small, community-minded country that had an incredibly low crime rate; I would have the security of Lesley and Pat close at hand, and it would help me along the road to self-sufficiency. It was the best decision I could have made.

The restaurant was to be called the Waterfront. From the moment I arrived there I didn't stop. There was everything to do. The restaurant had been built, but now it needed to be dec-orated, the chefs and staff employed, the menus planned, the suppliers appointed, an office organised and the launch public-ity planned. I was actually quite surprised – and very pleased – at how much responsibility I was given from the outset. The official opening was scheduled in six weeks' time, and I worked almost twenty-four hours a day until it arrived. I had no time to worry about whether I was capable or not, I just got on with it. This was exactly the kind of experience I needed.

I thrived on being able to use all my creative and hard-nosed buying skills. I had enjoyed the excitement and pressures of setting it all up, and could now bask in the self-satisfaction of seeing my various new business initiatives come to fruition.

Once the restaurant was up and running I found the hours were just as long. We had to cater for visiting tourists during the day and the late-night eating habits of the Spanish. The work became monotonous. The challenge had gone, and I was ready for a new one.

This came, quite unexpectedly, in the form of two letters: one from Valerie and one from Heather and Chip. Valerie had handed in her notice at Sears and was planning a six-month round-the-world trip. This was something we used to day-dream about, but never thought would actually happen. Heather and Chip were planning their trip to India. Seeing India was something I had always wanted to do, and it would give me the chance to visit the birthplaces of Mum and Dad. Valerie and Chip and Heather were all planning to leave in September, and were inviting me to come with them. As much as I wanted to do this trip, I didn't want to be a gooseberry either! Valerie had a new man in her life, and he would be meeting her at various points on her trip; Heather and Chip were together, and I definitely didn't feel this was the kind of trip I could handle on my own.

After much soul-searching, and all the inoculations, I declined to go with anyone. I wanted to travel but if I was going to do this on my own I needed something closer to home first. So, one year after arriving in Gibraltar, I set off to tour America.

Meeting Ali in New York was the first and most important

stop. We had a lot of catching up to do. When I was attacked he was unable to leave New York to see me and, later, I was unable to travel to see him, so we had to communicate by letter and phone.

I spent a week with him, went to work with him, did everything with him. Ali was like a brother to me and the happiness I felt in his company served only to intensify my love of New York City. However, I had never really seen much of the country outside of New York State. So I planned an East to West Coast trip with one of my American friends. This would form the first leg of my trip. The second would centre on visiting all my friends on the way back to New York. I felt that I was now ready to do this on my own.

I flew to Chicago and met my friend Nick. From there we went by car, alongside the legendary Route 66, and took in plenty of open roads, not to mention some famous sights, to reach our destination. The sheer scale of the wide open spaces seemed to give me the space I needed to think about my life and what I really wanted to get out of it. Once in LA we met up with our own friends and went our separate ways. I spent the next few weeks visiting my friends' homes in San Francisco, El Paso, Mexico and Santa Fe. These were people that I hadn't seen since the attack and cared about dearly. Although we did very normal touristy things together, it was a very special and emotional time for all of us.

On arrival back in New York I found out that Sharon was pregnant with baby number three, and I was stricken with homesickness. Eventually I returned to England. I'd been away six months. So much for my travel bug!

I wasn't the same person though. I felt I was much stronger, much more independent and much more focused. I knew what I wanted to do with my future.

As a child I always believed I was destined for a career in sport. By a strange twist of fate what was supposed to be a sporting career became one in fashion. Fashion no longer had the cachet for me and, to be frank, it now seemed very trivial after what I had been through.

I followed my heart and went back to my first love: sport. I am developing my career in that direction, just as Dad had always hoped.

I am now a qualified aerobics and fitness instructor and also teach 'personal safety for everyday life'. I feel pleased with my achievements, but it has not been without problem.

In putting my self-preservation first, I have inadvertently destroyed some of the friendships that were so important to me and my recovery. I regret that, but I hope those people will understand that the attack plucked me out of my place in life and I have spent the past five years trying to make my own way back. I don't know when I'll get there, I just know I will.

From my earliest memories I have always had a 'best friend'; a girlfriend who was my confidante, my sounding board, my constant companion. For the first time in my life I don't have one, and I feel the absence keenly.

I have had several relationships over the past five years, but they have not lasted. In most cases I have found that my partners have been unable to cope with what happened to me. Yet I believe that has more to do with them and their psyche than me. I have completely blanked Ferrira from my emotions. As far as I am concerned he evokes neither hatred nor forgiveness in me.

If I am to blame anyone for my failure to meet and form any kind of lasting bond with men, I must blame my dad. He is my benchmark as far as caring and friendship is concerned. I don't know what my psychiatrist would make of this, but essentially I have always craved the security and unconditional love he gave me. Now I am lucky enough to find these elusive elements in Andrew.

Andrew runs his own design consultancy in the City of London and, for over eight years, we have had the same circle of friends. Naturally our paths crossed regularly, but it was only in 1996 that we realised our relationship went beyond being 'just good friends'. I am happier now than I have been for many years. It has been a long, hard struggle to reach this point where I feel confident, fulfilled and loved, and despite what I have been through, I wouldn't swap places with anyone in the world.

I have met many brave people since 1992, and I never cease to marvel at their resilience, at their ability to overcome the worst the world has thrown at them.

Knowing them has helped me write this book. Now I can cross it off my list, and present my story to you in the hope that it will make a difference.

APPENDIX 1

Sharon's Story

Saturday, 15 February was the start of a very disturbing week. Loraine and Danny had come down from Manchester to spend the weekend with us. Saturday was going to be a mooching-around-London day and Sunday was for visiting relatives in Bedford. Merlyn was living in Tulse Hill and so travelled over early on Saturday morning to be with all of us. When she arrived, the rest of the household was enjoying something called 'deep sleep' but when you are the mother of a two-year-old, as I am, 'deep sleep' is merely a very pleasant, very distant memory. I made tea and we chatted until slowly the others came to and uncurled to face the day.

We were going to window-shop in Camden. Although I had lived there for seven years, there was always something new to see. And if we were going to do any sort of shopping at all, winter was the best time to do it, avoiding all those coaches belching out be-shorted, camera-clicking tourists. It was also possible to get a table in one of our favourite restaurants in Delancey Street without having to wait. We decided to walk into town and 'do' Camden High Street first, break for lunch and then go on to Camden Lock. 'We' consisted of myself and baby Merlyn, Loraine and Danny and sister Merlyn.

John made his excuses, as he always did, and waved us off. It was around 11.30 a.m. Bliss was written all over his face as we turned the corner leading into Camden Square. I could mentally picture him pouring himself another cup of strong tea, settling his tall frame into the leather armchair, putting his feet up and reading the newspaper from cover to cover. I momentarily chided myself for feeling jealous of John. I knew only too well that, given the luxury of a few uninterrupted hours of peace, I'd fill them with something 'useful' like cleaning out a cupboard. I just haven't got the hang of taking it easy yet.

It was a pleasant enough day, bright with a slight chill in the air. Camden Town was a good fifteen minutes of brisk walking away. Once we hit Camden High Street we split up: Danny and Loraine went in search of sports shops, Merlyn to look at clothes, and I pressed on with baby Merlyn and the buggy to Boots. The agreement was that we would all meet up outside Boots before going to lunch.

I guess I must have completed my shopping way ahead of the others because I seemed to be waiting quite a long time for them. I had crouched down by the buggy to have a chat with my daughter to prevent us both from becoming bored. Gradually I became aware of a far-off beat; a rhythmic drumming noise. I shut my eyes momentarily to listen without distraction. The beat was getting closer and sounded more urgent.

Before I had time to realise what was going on, about fifty young men in jeans and T-shirts were running in the road towards me, chanting something almost indistinguishable, but it sounded like 'Kill the bastards'. To say they looked menacing is to put it mildly, but I couldn't take my eyes off this rabble as they were approaching. I slowly got up and pushed Merlyn back inside Boots. Once this was done, the security guard pulled down the security grille and locked us all in. There were quite a few of us taking refuge in Boots, but no one said a word. We were either too frightened to talk, or transfixed as more and more men, no, yobs, were racing towards their destination. I glanced down the road and there running behind them, wide-eyed, ashen-faced but determined, was Loraine. What on earth did she think she was doing? The men reached the World's End pub at the top of the road where Camden High Street divides into Chalk Farm Road and Camden Road, and then proceeded to take it apart with a violence that was indescribable. The sound of smashing glass was terrifying, but then it stopped almost as quickly as it had started, and the men ran off in all directions.

It took a matter of seconds for Hell to come and go. It took minutes for the police to arrive, but by that time all that remained for them to question was something that resembled a disaster area.

By the time Loraine drew level with Boots the trouble had thankfully passed and the security grille lifted. I was angry with her for putting herself in such danger, but she had been worried about me and my baby, and reckoned it was worth the risk.

With the exception of my intrepid sister Loraine, we had all managed to hide in various shops. None of us had ever encountered raw brutality at such close quarters and we all felt quite shaky. We went to the restaurant, to calm our nerves more than anything else, had a light lunch and went home. The day was ruined, but we hadn't been harmed. Little did anyone realise at the time that this was a presage of something far worse.

The next morning we set off for our Aunty Sheila's house in Bedford. We spent a great day walking, chatting, eating. It was marvellously relaxed and gossipy, and none of us wanted the day to end. Aunty Sheila had been Daddy's best friend, apart from being his elder sister, and she was still able to tell us things about him that we didn't know. To a certain extent we still thirst for more knowledge about him and about Mummy.

On Sunday evening we all went our separate ways. I was employed as a Communications Consultant by a marketing communications company in Fulham. Merlyn rang me at the office on Monday morning to tell me she had an important meeting with one of her directors the next day, and would I like to take over her hair appointment at Trevor Sorbie's in Covent Garden, as she needed to prepare for the meeting. I had commitments myself, so had to decline. So, the next morning she was running late, missed the bus she normally took to work, and ended up walking to Brixton tube station. Had I said 'yes' things might have worked out very differently.

The police arrived at my company's reception that Tuesday and asked for me. They then asked if they could have a private chat with me. As I was showing them into the lift to take us to one of the conference rooms, I kept wondering what I had done wrong. I knew that they had called at my house, because my au pair had just telephoned me. Why do we always feel so guilty when the police are around? I kept trying to lighten the atmosphere by cracking jokes about parking tickets. All they could do was give me half-hearted smiles and then stare at their feet, as the interminably slow lift chugged to the top floor. I thought then that I must be in big trouble, but what?

Sergeant Simon Seeley broke the news to me that my sister Merlyn had been mugged, no, stabbed, no, raped, well, stabbed and raped, by one man, but it could be two. My hand went to my chest to prevent my heart bursting through it. Then I began to cry. The news was too awful. I tried to ask questions, but every time I did, I'd break down again. They were trying to calm me down and give me more information at the same time, but I just wanted to get to the hospital and be with Merlyn. I knew she'd need me, and I needed to see her. I was standing up and halfway out of the conference room when I think they realised they would have to cover everything else on the way. They told me she was in hospital in south London and they would take me there now.

Once in the police car I felt more composed and asked the other police officer to tell me a little more. PC Carroll was actually the first policeman to be on the scene and comforted Merlyn while waiting for help to arrive. Stupidly I asked whether she had any clothes on, and when he said no, I started crying yet again. I was inordinately concerned with the fact that numerous people might have seen her naked, and that she might have been feeling really embarrassed. He told me he covered her with his jacket and I felt relieved.

The car journey was fast and torturous. With siren blaring, lights flashing and wheels screeching we covered the few miles between south west London and south east London in record time. It slowly dawned on me that there must be a reason for needing to get me there so fast. I asked the one question I never thought I'd have to ask: is my sister alive? Seeley and Carroll exchanged looks and Seeley replied, 'We think so.'

The car stopped directly outside the ambulance entrance to Casualty and I was struggling to get out of the car with my seat belt on. Sergeant Seeley leaned over and said that he understood Merlyn had had no ill effects from the smoke inhalation. I stopped struggling and stared at him. I now know he was trying to comfort me with that information, but as I hadn't known about any fire I was unprepared. All I could think was that 'they'd' burned my beautiful baby sister.

I spent the rest of the day just holding her hand. We've always been a very tactile family, and I believed that physical contact was very important to both of us at that moment. I refused to make any phone calls except the very necessary ones, so I was hardly away from her side except for the briefest of moments.

When the time came for her operation, the doctors assured me she would be in surgery for several hours. John took me home so I could make those phone calls that would turn the rest of my family's lives upside down. He stayed with me as I made each call, and took over each time I broke down. I didn't make a good job of this particular piece of communication.

When the hospital rang two hours later to say that Merlyn was out of theatre, I was astonished. This was hardly 'several' hours, so she must have been in better shape than they had originally thought. I was torn. I wanted to be with Merlyn when she woke up, but I needed to make more calls. The media had gone haywire about the attack, and there was extensive coverage on television, radio and in the evening papers. I didn't want our family and friends hearing about Merlyn that way. My daughter could sense something had changed, and I didn't want to panic her in any way by disappearing when she felt unsettled.

I stayed. To this day I regret not being at the hospital. I should have been there when she first opened her eyes.

It was a long night for us. All the phone calls had been made, but now people were ringing me back. Mainly to talk. Sometimes to have me repeat what I'd said earlier because they didn't, couldn't, believe their own ears.

John and I had to be at the hospital early the next morning, so decided to get a few hours' sleep. I was completely exhausted, but just couldn't fall asleep. Once I'd decided sleep was impossible, I gave up the fight and went to make myself a cup of tea.

The house was in total darkness, but I wanted the stillness and the peace that this darkness gave me. I sank down into John's comfy leather armchair, hugged my knees into my chest and went through the events of that Tuesday. Merlyn had told the police and me exactly what had happened to her during the attack, and I found the news almost too much to bear. I rested my head on my knees and cried until there were no tears left.

What happened to Merlyn robbed her of her innocence, and tinged the hearts of all of us who love her with a deep and abiding sadness. But as the show must always go on, I have continued to live my life as 'normal'. The past five years haven't been easy, though. My outward strength and determination just camouflages my inner weaknesses. I feel less capable, less able to cope and I compensate for that by working ever harder to prove myself wrong.

Merlyn has recovered well, but I'm not sure she will ever recover completely. The way she has dealt with adversity is, however, an inspiration to everyone I know, and I'm sure to thousands of others. Her resulting lust for life is astounding and puts my efforts to shame.

In the early days Merlyn's friend Valerie suggested that I should have counselling. I thought about it, and thought it was probably a good idea. I've just never found the time to do it.

Five years on I still cry a lot and always in the dark or where no one can see me. I think of it as a kind of ongoing mourning.

Nicky's Story

I parked my car at the back of the police station at around 1.45 that afternoon. By the time I got to the 'office' it was nearer 2 p.m., the start of my late turn.

It had been a quiet February so far, and I wasn't expecting much action that day, so I was surprised when a senior officer told me to get straight over to King's College Hospital to attend a rape victim. I was still in my civvies, and about to fly out of the door of the station, when he came after me and told me where it happened, and when.

That was it. That was all the information I was given. When I got to the hospital I managed to get the briefest of details from one of the nursing staff and she pointed out Merlyn's sister Sharon to me. She was speaking quietly on the staff telephone so I had to wait until she had finished. The ward was very quiet, tranquil almost. The sunshine flooding through the windows made me feel so peaceful I could have curled up in one of the beds – had there been an empty one. When Sharon had finished, I went up to her and introduced myself. She acted as if she had been expecting me, and showed me straight into Merlyn's room.

The sight that met me when I entered that room was indescribable. I had never witnessed injuries on this scale before – and never have since. By rights she should have been dead. I was horrified at the extent of the wounds. Her face was so disfigured that it was impossible to tell what she might have looked like. (I have since admitted to Sharon privately that I initially thought that underneath all the cuts, bruises and swelling lay a very unattractive lady!)

I had been asked to question Merlyn because I had received specialist SOIT (Sexual Offences Investigation Techniques) training. But nothing in the training had prepared me for this. I knew I needed to get a rudimentary statement from Merlyn to help the investigating team, but as Merlyn could only speak softly, I had to get quite close. Being that close it was hard to ignore the wounds, and it was hard not to be amazed at her lucidity too. I was desperately trying to concentrate on what Merlyn had to say, but now I was beginning to feel slightly faint. When I thought I had enough information I left the room to phone it through. When I got outside the room I must have looked visibly distressed, because one of the nurses asked me if I was all right. I said I thought I might pass out, so she pointed to a chair in the distance. Looking at the chair was as near as I could get to it before passing out cold on the hospital floor.

From the word go I developed a very strong bond with Merlyn. It could have been due to the fact that we were both the same age, both single and very independent. I was very clear about my professional responsibilities, and didn't want my involvement with Merlyn to compromise them. Nevertheless, once you got to know Merlyn it was very hard not to become heavily involved.

Two days after meeting her I had to take a very detailed statement from her about the attack. It took two whole days to complete and left Merlyn mentally and physically exhausted. I found the two days of hearing about her assailant's savagery harrowing. When I got home after the second day I fell into a deep sleep. That was when my nightmares began. For two months I was plagued by the same nightmare: I was reliving the trauma of Merlyn's attack as though I was her. It was hard to carry on as if nothing was happening, but I really didn't want anyone to know what I was experiencing. They wouldn't understand. By bottling up my feelings about them, the nightmares only got worse, more vivid. After a while I decided to take a leaf from her book and talked to a few close friends about it. It helped more than I can say.

This case touched everyone on the force and galvanised the whole team working on it. If a man could do this to an innocent young woman with absolutely no provocation, he would do it again. We had to catch him, and we had to look after Merlyn. Everyone seemed to care about what happened to Merlyn. If she wanted something, nothing was too much trouble for any of us. Somehow we were all taking this attack personally. When a few of us went to the dump at Mucking in Essex to search for some of Merlyn's belongings, it was like looking for a needle in a giant haystack. But we were happy to do it. To do it for Merlyn.

The same went for Merlyn too. Whatever we wanted from her, we got. Nothing was too much trouble.

I found that I was worrying about her too. She had suffered so much, yet she felt she had to be strong for the rest of her family. It was as if she didn't want to distress them any further by showing her own distress. I felt it was important for me to be there for her as her outside release.

To be trusted by her, I had to be trusted by her family. She was so close to all her sisters, and they had formed a very potent security ring around her. Fortunately they all accepted me very quickly, and I became an honorary member of the Nuttall family. There were many high points and low points for me during the investigation, but I reached the lowest point of all when Merlyn couldn't pick Ferrira out in the line-up. Everyone on the team was banking on a positive ID, and we were all totally devastated when she failed to give one. It was a big day for her. She knew how much the identification meant to the case, but she was also petrified of seeing him again.

I became very frustrated with the case once Ferrira had been arrested and was awaiting trial. I didn't feel the evidence we had was strong enough, yet the enquiry was closed down. I knew the evidence was out there, and felt I had to make an effort to uncover it.

One of the funniest things that happened to me while I was doing this was when I was at Jeanette's flat. Apart from being Ferrira's girlfriend, she was also a prostitute. On one particular occasion we were discussing his sexual past, but as her vocabulary wasn't exactly encyclopaedic, she had to resort to physically showing me a particular position. While she was contorting herself, she looked up at me and said, 'Wouldn't your DI like to see you now!'

When the trial was over we were all in party mood. Merlyn, her family and friends and the key players on the investigating team could now let our hair down. It was quite usual for us to celebrate after such a victory; what was unusual was the fact that we were all doing it together. The bond that had been forged between us over the past few months was incredibly strong. I think we all treasure that.

I was in awe of Merlyn's courage and I still am. It made me realise how very trivial many of my own problems are.

Working on this case was good for me. I learned so much. What counted for me, however, was that at the end of the day I felt I made a difference.

Valerie's Story

Work was manic, so when Sharon left a message for me to call her I didn't do so straight away.

Finally I dialled the number she'd left. It wasn't her home number, so I presumed she must be calling from a meeting. I hoped I hadn't missed her. Unexpectedly I got through to a hospital ward, but within a few seconds John was on the line telling me that Merlyn had been attacked. From the way he spoke, I wasn't sure she was alive.

I left work immediately.

Once I reached the hospital one of the nurses directed me to Merlyn's room. The light was off but I could see that it was completely empty. There was not even a bed in it. Then I became aware of Sharon and John sitting on the floor in one corner. I didn't want to think the worst but it was difficult not to.

Apparently Merlyn was in the operating theatre. As Sharon filled me in on the day's events, a nurse told us Merlyn could be in surgery for several hours. It was suggested we go home until we were needed. In the quiet of my flat, the reality of the situation sank in. I couldn't quite believe it had happened. It seemed too unreal. I desperately wanted to see Merlyn again.

The phone call came much earlier than expected; it could only have been a couple of hours since I had been at the hospital. Sharon and John had to stay at home, so at least I'd be with Merlyn. Not knowing what to expect I went straight into her room. No one stopped me; in fact I didn't see a soul.

The light was on this time, and I honestly couldn't believe my eyes. Merlyn was unrecognisable.

She couldn't move her head very easily, but detected I was there. She smiled. She didn't look like the Merlyn I knew so well. Her eyes were badly disfigured and distended, but I could still see that they were Merlyn's eyes. We talked and talked and slowly she became more and more euphoric. I imagine that she was beginning to realise how lucky she was to be alive.

We talked into the early hours of the next day and she told me everything. It was almost as if by telling me, her memory of it wouldn't disappear. She was trying to keep it clear for the police. She talked herself to sleep. At six that morning Sharon and John arrived, and I left for work.

At first I didn't mention anything about Merlyn to my colleagues at work. However, eventually they realised, especially when they saw the newspapers and the reconstruction on television. Many people had met her. It affected them all.

The potential dangers were brought home to all the women at work, so I arranged for the local police to visit our offices and give talks on how to protect ourselves in situations like Merlyn's.

I spent some time with Merlyn in Spain and there was no doubt the rest and the climate were helping.

When Merlyn returned to England we still spent time

together but things were changing. My life continued as before but, as is to be expected after such a traumatic incident, Merlyn's was never going to be the same.

We had a very intense friendship and I tried very hard to rationalise why it was no longer working. Perhaps I reminded her too much of this tragic event. Whatever it was, I now realised that I was of no use to her any more, and that hurt.

We still keep in touch, but it's not like it was before.

The day *he* entered her life was the beginning of the end of our friendship – but Merlyn is alive and that's all that really matters.

The Psychiatrist's View:

Professor Robert Cawley

Merlyn Nuttall came to see me on 28 May 1992. Well-groomed, articulate and charming, she talked with controlled anxiety about recent events in her life. She described the assault that she had endured three months earlier: abduction at knife-point, degrading sexual abuse, near-strangling with cheese wire, multiple cuts with broken glass, burns sustained during attempted incineration, and her eventual escape, naked, into a world which at first sight seemed to be looking in the opposite direction. The arrival of the fire brigade, a fireman's recognition that she was losing blood and in extremis, the press of questions by the police, the long wait for the ambulance. The gentleness of the firemen and police, the ordeal of the forensic examination, the relief when her beloved and loving sister arrived, the stark terror of knowing that the assailant was at liberty, perhaps to try to renew his attack. Six days in hospital, departure for Spain ten days later, ten weeks' attempt at recuperation there with another sister, and her return to London two weeks earlier.

It was a deeply moving interview. Such a first meeting with a patient was unique in my thirty years experience as a psychiatrist: unsurpassed as a first-hand account of an extremity of violence and of death averted only by resourcefulness, delivered in measured terms and with much composure. In her every word she acknowledged the intensity of the distress which had altered everything in her life, yet she was firm in asserting her foremost feeling – of gratitude that she was still alive and, in essentials, intact.

How, I wondered, can one survive such an experience? That was perhaps the first time I learned what a very considerable distance separates the concepts of victim and survivor. Here was an obviously unusual person, a victim of hideous violence, whose life and undoubted future owed everything to her possessing the thoughts, attitudes and behaviour of a survivor. A survivor: one who under duress gains strength by looking to the future. That was the lesson Merlyn taught me on our first meeting, and I have been moved and delighted subsequently to learn that she intends to devote part of her future to extending what she has learned from her experiences to a wider audience. I am honoured to be invited to write a brief appendix to her book.

And so I learned what had happened to Merlyn, and saw that she was a survivor. I do not mean to imply that she was not suffering, and that she was able to brush aside the consequences of her ordeal. Far from it: she well recognised, and conveyed, her own insecurity and fear. She was much aware of the uncertainties that had entered her life: the trepidations, and the compelling avoidances necessitated for the sake of going forward from day to day.

She knew that for the foreseeable future she would not be able to live alone. There was no question of using public transport. She could go nowhere without her personal telephone. Her life was diminished by fear. She was no longer able to be a young professional woman relishing her autonomy and looking forward to career developments, the realisation of ambitions, adventure, love, marriage and children. These familiar confident vistas of a welcoming future were obliterated by the prospect of a distinctively defensive lifestyle. She had to take her leave of the independent life, defer plans, and tread warily into a world racked with uncertainty. Moreover she would have to undergo extensive plastic surgery for the scars on her neck, and physiotherapy for her injured right hand. And she would have to go to court, perhaps to the committal trial of her assailant, and certainly to be a witness at the substantive trial. There were very real horrors which she would have to live through, which could threaten to reactivate the engulfing nightmare through which she had passed. She knew the dangers she was in, recognised her own vulnerability, and accepted the pain of her predicament. She had insight, and my impression was that she would not be able to accept anything less than ruthless honesty with herself.

Merlyn was planning to re-establish herself at work on a part-time basis ten days after seeing me for the first time. We talked about our further meetings. She felt safe and cared for by her family and was concerned to get on with the tasks of her new lifestyle. She had to attend her physiotherapist and her plastic surgeon and she hoped to start seeing some of her friends. She wanted to regain her old life within the limits of what was possible and this would require all her time and courage and strength. She knew what she had to do, and recognised that only she herself could run the race. I hoped she was reassured to know that she could see me at short notice whenever she wished.

In fact four months elapsed before our second meeting. Again she appeared to be in remarkably good shape. She was receiving much support from her family and from colleagues at work. She was expecting to have to attend her assailant's trial at the Old Bailey as a witness a few weeks hence. Of course she was particularly dreading this, and felt burdened by the disadvantage of being the voiceless victim, since the law is such that she was not allowed to have an advocate on the prosecution side. The police were being helpful and understanding. She had arranged to have treatment with a sympathetic and sensitive plastic surgeon. I wrote in my notes that she was physically well, virtually free from overt symptoms, though far from recovered from the effects of the assault: the fear remained and her life continued to be restricted, and moreover she was facing further painful events which could provoke a delayed emotional reaction.

However she did not return until a further four months had passed, in February 1993. Again she was smart and very composed. The trial had been postponed until a date three weeks previously. There had followed a period of celebration with many friends, and a sympathetic interview reported in the *Evening Standard*, following which a number of friendly strangers had written to her. The general advice had been that she could now put the horrors behind her and get on with her life. However she admitted to a sense of anticlimax. She had been feeling a bit unclear about what there was to celebrate, and she expressed some uncertainties and bewilderment on having come to the end of a painful year culminating with the Old Bailey trial. Her work as a buyer had begun to pall, and she was not sure what her next move might be. She was floundering and felt she had lost her drive. She could not do as so many people were advising and forget all about the pain and the memory. What had happened could not be effaced. She had decided to write a book about the assault and its human consequences. In the meantime, she felt absolutely uncertain about her short- and long-term plans. My two pieces of advice were that she should not be in a hurry to make any firm commitments, and that she should attend for a course of weekly sessions with a very skilled and experienced counsellor, a colleague of mine whom I here refer to as Margaret.

Merlyn accepted both parts of this advice and came to see Margaret every week – and later every two weeks – for eighteen months, until she left for Gibraltar in August 1994. This was Merlyn's substantive treatment, and I myself remained in the background and saw her at intervals of about six weeks. It was the time during which she made such impressive progress towards freeing herself from the fear and the restraints and recovering her independence. She became progressively more confident and at ease with herself. She changed her employment but had, rather reluctantly, moved to Essex in order to continue to live with her sister and brother-in-law and niece. She resumed regular exercise – badminton, tennis and aerobics – and lost 20lb in weight, feeling she had returned to the peak of physical fitness she had known before the attack. She began to crave a return to her life in London. Her ideas of writing about her experiences matured over this period. She had begun to talk about them more publicly, and had been invited to speak to the Home Affairs Committee of the Bow Group in the House of Commons. In August 1994 she moved to Gibraltar, and a year later she left for an extended period in the United States.

After her return I saw her in August 1996. From what she said and from her manner it was clear that she had made remarkable progress along the road to recovery, and had enjoyed a life which included a period of innovative work, travel and companionship, and serious thought about developing a new career. The past was far more firmly established as the past, but of course it was by no means forgotten.

It is a universal truth that severe injury, or trauma, consciously experienced, is damaging to the mind, just as it can be to the body. The symptoms of the mind's distress consist in the first place of intense fear and horror, amounting to terror; at later stages the fear persists, and tends to be elaborated and accompanied by feelings, thoughts and behaviour depending in some way on the nature of the trauma. Merlyn's experience, with its extremes of degradation, torture, and threat of dying, understandably caused lasting fear which in many ways distorted her life for years after the event, and continues to influence her. She has described this herself. Her principal reactions to fear – in its early days and subsequently – took the form of conscious avoidance of many situations she had come to see as dangerous. She avoided being alone and removed herself from the locality, and even, at first, from the country. She sought only the company of those she loved and trusted, and virtually isolated herself from her previous life and relationships. As time passed, she began to make increasingly strenuous efforts to go through various stages towards a return to the realities of her previous life. She is now planning to re-establish herself in a new home of her own in London.

In biological terms, Merlyn has been through successive stages of an adaptive process. During the assault her decision to feign death can be seen as an adaptation to enormous threat, and one which probably saved her life. Afterwards she adapted to trauma by withdrawing from those aspects of her life which she saw as potentially threatening, and seeking security and a caring environment. The adaptive process continued as her ability to come out of hiding reasserted itself. And, let it be noted, she has had to adapt not only to the original trauma but to a series of secondary traumas – hospitalisation and operations, the identification parade, the trial, the unwelcome attentions of the media, the institutionalised offensiveness of the proceedings of the Criminal Injuries Compensation Board, the estrangement from friends, the feelings of alienation; and so on.

In medical terms, Merlyn has been suffering from a post-traumatic stress disorder (PTSD). Severe trauma characterised by terror was followed by fear, anxiety, withdrawal from situations perceived as threatening, and considerable social withdrawal, imposing painful limitations on her life. She became, in various ways, disabled and many of the activities of her life were compromised. She had to work very hard, with great courage, to rehabilitate herself.

Accounts of PTSD in the medical literature emphasise that in people suffering from the condition, symptoms and disabilities are determined by interaction of three sets of variables: (i) the personality and previous lifestyle; (ii) the nature and circumstances of the trauma; and (iii) what happens afterwards – the responses of other people to the injured person and the subsequent course of events. Merlyn was a successful professional woman living an independent and satisfying life and looking forward to a wide range and choice of personal and career developments. (However, it may be relevant that she had poignant experiences and memories of sadness, such as when her mother died when she was nine and when her father, especially important to her as she grew up, died three years before the trauma.) The nature of the trauma was as extreme as one could imagine, physically and psychologically: she was tortured and nearly killed, and exposed to a degree of terror which is barely comprehensible. After the event her treatment in hospital was competent and thereafter she was lovingly cared for in an environment made secure by her devoted family; she received continuing support from family and friends over four years, and she had eighteen months' skilled counselling. From this we can infer that the course of her illness was almost certainly helped by various aspects of her personality and previous lifestyle, and by the care she received after the event, although the trauma itself was such as to evoke a stress disorder of extreme severity.

Many people with PTSD experience a range of symptoms which represent elaborations of fear shaped (to an extent) by their psychological make-up including aspects of themselves of which they are not fully aware. There may be recurrent unbidden and distressing recollections of the event, with vivid 'flashbacks', distressing dreams related to the trauma, feelings that the event is recurring, and waves of severe psychological distress when the event is recalled. Often the sufferer persistently avoids thoughts, feelings, and conversation associated with the trauma. There may be an inability to recall important aspects of the trauma. Also, typically, there are symptoms of increased arousal – difficulty in falling or staying asleep, outbursts of irritability, difficulty in concentrating, increased startle responses. Other features may include guilt, feelings of ineffectiveness, shame, despair or hopelessness.

Merlyn experienced very little of these elaborations of fear and anxiety which are so commonly found in otherwise healthy people with PTSD. I was very struck by how vividly she was able to talk about the assault, and subsequent events, and I understand she talked freely about it to her family and others consistently from the first day. Her style was to be open and very honest with herself and those she confided in, and this I believe proved to be usefully adaptive in preventing the onset of certain symptoms and assisting her recovery. Her behaviour was not dominated by hidden fears because virtually all her fears seem to have been expressed. She had no more than a single flashback (provoked by going into a room with a skylight and a layout similar to the scene of the attack). She did not have insomnia: on the contrary her sleep requirement temporarily increased from her normal five hours a night to eight. She had no nightmares but deliberately 'turned over the matter' (her expression) day and night. Her restricted social functioning was under her own conscious and reasoned control. She modified her activities according to what she considered logical and sensible. Her way of dealing with her short-term future was, from the start, pragmatic. And she was always consciously, and uncomfortably, aware of her anxiety. It was never denied or expressed significantly by indirect means. She had unflinching insight, and this is (to the observer) always a good sign.

Merlyn was also unusual, compared with most people diagnosed with post-traumatic stress disorder, in that the decision to have counselling was not made until relatively late after the trauma. It is often held that the earlier counselling starts, the better will be the prospect of a good recovery. In Merlyn's case three months passed before her first consultation. Before then she had been occupied with her hospital admission and with removing herself to another country where she would feel safe and be looked after. During all this time she was talking freely about the assault with her sisters and others she could trust. After her return, at the time of her first consultation, she was very occupied with the practicalities of gradually returning to living in sheltered circumstances in London, and working; her continuing physical treatment, and getting through the preparation for the trial and the trial itself. She was also reflecting deeply on her past experiences and present predicament and, with everything else, might have felt that she had enough on her plate. It was only after the trial that she and I recognised that a period of formal counselling was highly desirable. This sequence of events is unusual, but understandable; it is certainly the case that the timing of counselling is all-important, and perhaps an early start is usually, but by no means always, propitious. Moreover, from the very day of the assault, the support which is one component of the best counselling was provided to great effect by her family.

At the trial of her assailant, the Judge was reported as saying, 'She is a woman of great courage and a strong personality, and this, one hopes, has helped her face her injuries and the consequences of that dreadful ordeal.' Those comments could be underpinned by volumes of psychological theorising, but their cogency could not be surpassed. Merlyn is fortunate in having inherited and acquired what it takes to achieve a rather unusual combination of mental balance, understanding, intelligence and courage: though deeply unfortunate in losing her mother when she was nine, and immensely saddened by her father's death when she was twenty-four, she was extremely fortunate in having three loving sisters and some very good friends. Circumstances of great good fortune have helped her to find the resolve and determination to survive and overcome a hideous assault for which she was a random victim. In medical terms she has certainly recovered. It looks as if she has survived the event and overcome the human consequences as much as is humanly possible. She has much to teach us because she has vividly demonstrated the knack of looking to the future as an aid to surviving the present. Her story is an affirmation of the human spirit, and also tells us much about the value and uses of facing unpalatable truth and mental pain without becoming dismayed and defeated, however great the fears, hardship and costs to oneself. She is indeed a survivor.

In the course of her long voyage of return to normal life, Merlyn has reflected deeply on the aftermath of being a victim including the many secondary insults, often unwitting, from individuals and institutions, the law's delays, the intrusiveness of the media, and even from friends whose concern and compassion may somehow impede communication. She has developed a remarkable understanding of the human consequences of severe trauma. I see this book as an emblem of her determination to turn misfortune to advantage. What she has to say will, I believe, be of inestimable value to many people, among them those who meet with violent crime personally, their families and others who help them, and those who work with them professionally.

Robert Cawley

Survivor's Guide

When you, or someone you know, becomes the victim of a violent crime, you will need a lot of support. Unfortunately all too often you may find that you suffer yet again, but this time at the hands of those who are actually there to help.

I have written this aide-memoire as a result of my experiences over the past five years. It is unlikely to change legislation, but it will help you get the best from the services that are there to support you.

Its very essence is about taking charge. You may be too unwell to affect anything, but that should not prevent a close relative or friend from doing things on your behalf. You deserve the very best there is, but sometimes *you* have to make it happen.

At the Crime Scene

- However horrible the attack has been, you are going to feel better with someone you know nearby. Tell the police who to contact. This does not have to be a family member, but it should be someone you trust and, preferably, someone who is used to getting things done.

Who to Call

- You, of course, may not be able to (or want to) ring anyone after the attack, and that is your prerogative. Get your friend to do it. Your family and friends will be worried about you and will want to help. Use them. You may have children that need to be looked after, pets that need to be fed or walked, a house to be secured.

- If your personal belongings have been stolen your bank must be informed immediately. The police can do this for you, but you may need to discuss other financial matters with your bank manager so you can get through this traumatic period comfortably. If you can't do it, ask your friend.

In Hospital

- The staff will do everything in their power to save your life and stabilise your condition, but don't be so grateful that you don't want to bother them should some other symptoms manifest themselves later. They may have missed something, so let them know about it.

- The forensic medical examiner will then be allowed, with your permission, to take samples from your body for forensic examination. Don't assume that he/she will do everything right. Play safe and ask for another doctor to be present. If you are a girl or woman, you may feel easier having a female doctor present, especially if the forensic medical examiner is male, so ask for one.

- You will not be feeling on top form, so if things aren't going right for you, you may not be able to do very much about it. Enlist the help of your friend. Let him or her be your mouthpiece. (We all seem able to fight other people's corners far better than our own.)

- The hospital staff are not a security service, but if you feel you are at risk, tell them and they will tighten security on your ward, or call in the police if necessary.

- Before you leave, make the doctor spend time with you and, if needs be, provide detailed notes for you, so you are crystal clear on what treatment and aftercare you need and why. Check whether you will need to be screened for HIV and any other diseases. Communication between the hospital and your own GP may not be as efficient as you'd like to think – this is your last chance to get the information.

- If you have to return to outpatients for a consultation, ask for an appointment outside the normal hours. The hospital, or the area itself, may hold lots of bad memories for you, and the last thing you should be subjected to is a crowded waiting room for hours. You are bound to meet with a certain amount of resistance over such a request, but most people are understanding and would not want to increase your already great suffering.

- If you are not satisfied with your treatment, get a second opinion quickly. You mustn't wait too long, or the damage may become irreversible.

The Police

- If you can give them as much information as possible directly after the attack it will help. Don't hold anything back. You never know how important a seemingly useless detail may be.

- A trained liaison officer will be appointed to you. If you don't get on with him/her, say so. You need a link to the police investigation, but you must feel that he/she has your best interests at heart.

The Line-up

- Remember your assailant will do everything in his/her power to change his/her appearance and look least like the person who assaulted you.

- Don't be rushed into making an identification by the police or your solicitor. It's better to be slow and right than fast and wrong.

- You may not be 100 per cent certain about someone, but rather than say nothing at all, voice an opinion there and then. It will go on record and it may help the case.

- If you need to hear his/her voice, ask to hear them all speak one by one. Your memory could be sparked by auditory recognition.

- You are bound to be nervous, traumatised even, so have someone accompany you to the line-up. They will not be able to walk along the line with you, but their presence may help to make you feel a little calmer.

The Trial

- Although you are the victim, you are only a witness in the eyes of the law. It will be the Crown who prosecutes your assailant. You will find that access to the solicitor and barrister working on the case is not always easily obtainable, no matter how hard you push. If you have to give very sensitive information to a packed courtroom, you have every right to meet the prosecuting barrister. If the police won't help you, contact the Crown Prosecution Service and quote the Victim's Charter at them.

- Going to court is likely to be a nerve-racking experience. Victim Support offer a service to take you to an empty courtroom, prior to your case, so that you will feel more at ease.

- When you eventually go, and this could be many months after the attack took place, you must confirm who will be escorting you. If you feel safer having the police around you rather than your family, say so.

- You don't know who you will meet when you get to court as there are so many public areas. Demand that you are taken to a private area to await your turn in the witness box. A private area means just that; not a canteen, not a corridor, not a loo.

Practical Help

- Being attacked is so horrific it is often pushed to the back of the mind, in a pretence that it doesn't exist, or in the hope that it might be forgotten. This won't help you in the long run. Acknowledging what has happened to you is extremely important. Talking about what happened to you may help; bottling it all up never will.

You may feel too embarrassed to talk to someone you know about the attack, or you may feel they couldn't handle it if they did know everything. Then you may need some sort of emotional support from another source. You may also need some fairly basic information too, but may be unsure where to turn for either.

You should contact the Victim Support National Centre on 0845 3030900 and they will let you know who your nearest Victim Support Contact is. They can offer practical help, such as filling in Criminal Injuries Compensation forms. If necessary, they can refer you to trained counsellors should you both agree it is needed. It is far better to seek help that will prevent a breakdown than to try and fix things once it has happened.

Employers

- Your employers should be contacted and informed. They may have schemes in place that will help you. It will put your mind at rest. If they don't, then you at least know where you stand and can make alternative arrangements.

Local Authorities

- You may be entitled to a disabled sticker or taxi discount card. Ask your local Social Services office what is available. Beware: this kind of information isn't always made easily available when your 'disability' is deemed to be a mental, rather than a physical one. Get advice from your doctor and Victim Support Contact before approaching them, so you don't blow your chances.

The Attack

- No one knows how they might react if they are attacked by someone. It's always a question of flight or fright. In my case I froze, and he was able to abduct me, at knifepoint, without too much fuss. If I had taken to my heels, or surprised him by screaming at the top of my voice because it was impossible to run, events might have turned out differently.

  I do realise now that by going to a secondary place of attack, namely a deserted top-floor room of a squat, I had drastically reduced my chances of ever being helped or discovered.